LOST AND FOUND

Reflections on the Prodigal Son

ROBERT L. MILLET

Illustrations by
James C. Christensen

DESERET
BOOK

SALT LAKE CITY, UTAH

Library of Congress Cataloging-in-Publication Data

Millet, Robert L.
  Lost and found : reflections on the prodigal son / Robert L. Millet.
    p.   cm.
  ISBN 1-57008-717-2 (alk. paper)
  1. Prodigal son (Parable)   2. Church of Jesus Christ of Latter-day Saints—Doctrines.   3. Mormon Church—Doctrines.   I. Title.
BT378.P8 .M535 2001
226.8'06—dc21   2001002679

Printed in the United States of America   72876-6849

10 9 8 7 6 5 4 3 2 1

CONTENTS

PREFACE

Many years ago I sat opposite a young man who had been on an extended spiritual detour. He had been brought up in the Church, had known many of the sweet fruits of faith in the Lord, had been nurtured along by caring advisers and teachers, and had for years lived a life that one would describe as worthy and commendable. But one compromise and omission led to another. He wandered from the strait path, lost his place in the Church, and opened himself and those who loved him to unspeakable tragedy and heartache.

Now, after almost ten years away from life in the Church and fellowship with the Saints, he had come to himself. He looked around, noticed just how far he had strayed, and was courageous enough to ask hard questions: Where am I? What has happened to me? What have I done? Is this what I thought it would be like? Am I happy? What can I do? Where can I turn? Is it possible to somehow make up for all the mischief and deception and sin I have spread? Will my family and friends even consider letting me return? Or is all lost?

After weeks of pondering and deep reflection, he decided simply to go home. Showing up unexpectedly at his parents' home, he called and asked to visit with me, his Church leader. We spoke of his sins, of the need for repentance, and of the miracle of forgiveness and renewal through the atonement of Jesus Christ. At a certain point in our conversation, he said with much fear and resignation, "I don't know if I can do this. I'm so far gone. The road back is so long."

I bore my testimony to him of the love of God, of the infinite and eternal atoning sacrifice of the Savior, and of my love for him and my willingness to walk beside him. As the days and weeks passed, we met together often. We read and applied the scriptures. We prayed. We fasted for strength. As the reality of the gospel, or the doctrine of Christ, began slowly to distil upon his soul, his hope for recovery and reconciliation began to grow. He spoke more and more often about coming back, about feeling and understanding what he had once felt and understood. The light of life, as found only in Jesus Christ (John 1:4, 9), began to shine in his countenance. His heart was changed. He had come home.

This book is about coming home, about straying souls who discover their plight and then, in a critical and vital moment, decide they do not want to live that way any more. They want to go home. Then begins the inner struggle: the doubts and fears, the worries and anxieties, the shame and embarrassment, all juxtaposed with the quiet but earnest hope that they will be loved and cared about and welcomed when they do arrive home.

The parable of the prodigal son is a story about a wandering son, about a "faithful" son, about a waiting father. It is a story about each of us as the prodigal son, for we "all have sinned, and come short of the glory of God" (Romans 3:23). It is a story about each of us as the older brother, for we must decide, at one time or another, how we will respond to the returning prodigal. And it is a story about each of us who aspires to godliness, for somewhere down the road of life, if we are serious about our Christian discipleship, we must choose to assume the role of the waiting father.

It is glorious and heartwarming to know that God our Father has a plan for his children, a plan of recovery, a plan of renewal and reconciliation, a plan of salvation, a plan by which those who wander—and that includes all of us—can pick ourselves up, dust ourselves off, and through the Atonement and the ordinances of salvation return home. Not one of us is bright enough or powerful enough to do it alone; we must have help. And were it not for divine assistance, each of us would falter and fail, would lose the battle of life. "But thanks be to God, which giveth us the victory through our Lord Jesus Christ" (1 Corinthians 15:57).

In the preparation of this manuscript, I am indebted to many persons. Members of the Religious Education faculty at Brigham Young University, as well as other colleagues in the Church Educational System, have asked good questions about this topic and made excellent suggestions. My long-time assistant, Lori Soza, has been, as always, efficient and thorough in her preparation of the manuscript for publication. Suzanne Brady of Deseret Book Company has made important editorial contributions to this book and offered invaluable recommendations for its improvement. But while I owe much to many, I alone am responsible for the views set forth in this book. Although I have tried to be true to the spirit and intent of the teachings of the scriptures and Church leaders, this work is a private endeavor and not an official publication of either The Church of Jesus Christ of Latter-day Saints or of Brigham Young University.

PART ONE

A certain man had

two sons: And the younger of

them said to his father, Father,

give me the portion of goods that falleth

to me. And he divided unto them his living.

INTRODUCTION

There is great value in being able to distil significant messages from a book of scripture or perhaps even from an important chapter or passage. So often we read through the scriptures—day in and day out, week after week and month after month, from start to finish—and do not take the time to step back, ponder, and reflect on the larger themes and doctrinal refrains that weave their way through the scriptures or the history of the Church.

I have found it especially helpful in teaching the Book of Mormon to returned missionaries, for example, to walk into class the first day and distribute copies of questions that will appear on the final examination. The students are generally stunned. They wonder why we would be contemplating the end in the beginning. Some of the questions I distribute include the following:

"Explain how the Book of Mormon is a 'history of a fallen people.'"

"Discuss how the Book of Mormon does indeed teach 'what great things the Lord hath done' for [our] fathers."

"Given more than a thousand years of history and experience within the pages of the Book of Mormon, what counsel would you offer to the rising generation on how to avoid the perils of the prosperity cycle?"

"Discuss the prophetic/editorial role of Mormon and how he helped to achieve the overarching purposes of the Book of Mormon."

"How do the Book of Mormon prophets establish in the minds of people in their day—as well as in our own time—that 'Jesus is the Christ, the Eternal God'?"

Questions like these cause us to think deeply and broadly, to embrace the specifics and assess the larger, more far-reaching messages they give us. They move us toward thinking comprehensively, toward viewing God and his gospel from a more elevated perspective.

When the risen Lord taught the Nephites assembled near the temple at Bountiful, he quoted passages of scripture from such prophets as Isaiah, Micah, and Malachi. He examined the Nephite records and found that the fulfillment of Samuel's prophecy concerning many Saints in America rising from the dead at the time of His resurrection had not been recorded. "And it came to pass that Jesus commanded that it should be written; therefore it was written according as he commanded."

Note what follows: "And now it came to pass that *when Jesus had expounded all the scriptures in one,* which they had written, he commanded them that they should teach the things which he had expounded unto them" (3 Nephi 23:13–14; italics added). He "expounded all the scriptures in one." What does that mean? What did the Master do?

A clue as to what the Lord was doing in America may be found in something he said and did in the Old World just after his resurrection. As he walked on the road to Emmaus with the two disciples—who did not recognize him—he listened to their animated conversation about the trial and crucifixion of Jesus of Nazareth: "But we trusted that it had been he which should have redeemed Israel: and beside all this, to day is the third day since these things were done." After hearing their description of the reports of the women and other disciples who found the tomb empty, the Savior chastened them for not making the connection, for not recognizing the week's events for what they were: "O fools, and slow of heart to believe all that the prophets have spoken: Ought not Christ to have suffered these things, and to enter into his glory?" (Luke 24:21, 25–26).

And then comes this revealing statement: "And beginning at Moses and all the prophets, he expounded unto them *in all the scriptures the things concerning himself*" (Luke 24: 27; italics added). That is, the Lord took occasion to bring together the Law, the Prophets, and the Writings, to distil their central message, to demonstrate how these sacred records all bear a united witness of him.

In the same way, we might distil the message of a specific book of scripture, such as Leviticus, by turning to a single verse: "The life of the flesh is in the blood . . . for it is the blood that maketh an atonement for the soul" (Leviticus 17:11). With all the numerous and varied details we encounter in Leviticus, including the many sacrificial offerings described in that rather difficult text, we are, through this verse, able to climb a hill and gain a better view of things. We may not be able to define or distinguish between burnt offerings, meal offerings, peace offerings, sin offerings, or trespass offerings, but we can begin to sense what is behind it all, what God would have us see and understand about the sufferings and death and atoning mercies of the Holy Messiah.

Think for a moment about the lengthy and complex allegory of Zenos in Jacob 5 in the Book of Mormon. In it we have a history of the world and a statement about the dealings of the Almighty with the nations of the earth. Reflect upon many of the symbols contained in this remarkable story: tame olive trees, wild olive trees, grafts, roots, branches, fruit, nethermost parts of the vineyard, servants, lord of the vineyard, and so forth. It is worthwhile to read and reread the allegory and seek as best we can to understand its detail, knowing that buried within is a treasure of inestimable worth, but we need not understand every symbol in Jacob 5 to grasp what the Lord is trying to teach us in that chapter.

Jacob offers in the next chapter his own perceptive commentary on the allegory when he glories in the Lord: "And how merciful is our God unto us, for he remembereth the house of Israel, both roots and branches; and he stretches forth his hands unto them all the day long. . . . Wherefore, my beloved brethren, I beseech of you in words of soberness that ye would repent, and come with full purpose of heart, and cleave unto God as he cleaveth unto you. And while his arm of mercy is extended towards you in the light of the day, harden not your hearts. . . . For behold, after ye have been nourished by the good word of God all the day long, will ye bring forth evil fruit, that ye must be hewn down and cast into the fire? Behold, will ye reject these words? Will ye reject the words of the prophets . . . ?" (Jacob 6:4–8). In short, God simply will not let Israel go!

In a very real way, what the world knows as the Golden Rule is a distillation of the message "Therefore all things whatsoever ye would that men should do to you, do ye even so to them: for this is the law and the prophets" (Matthew 7:12). Similarly, the Master identified "the great commandment in the law" as love: "Thou shalt love the Lord thy God with all thy heart, and with all thy soul, and with all thy mind. This is the first and great commandment. And the second is like unto it, Thou shalt love thy neighbour as thyself. On these two commandments hang all the law and the prophets" (Matthew 22:36–40). This royal law is "fulfilled in one word, even in this; Thou shalt love thy neighbour as thyself" (Galatians 5:14; see also James 2:8; Romans 13:9).

I am persuaded that Luke 15 is a distillation of the plan of salvation, a message within the Message, the gospel within the Gospel. The brief sermon of Luke 15 is deep and profound: God loves his children, all of them, and he will do everything in his power to save them. Joseph Smith pointed out that "while one portion of the human race is judging and condemning the other without mercy, the Great Parent of the universe looks upon the whole of the human family with a fatherly care and paternal regard; He views them as His off-spring, and without any of those contracted feelings that influence the children of men."[1]

Though not all who claim to be Christian agree about whether Jesus of Nazareth was the literal Son of God, whether he healed the sick and raised the dead, whether he had the power to remit sin and cleanse the human heart, or whether he rose from the dead and lives today, almost all Christians agree on one thing: Jesus loved people. Individuals may not acknowledge that he was divine, but they quickly confess that the documents portray Jesus as one who lifted and strengthened and built people.

There is, however, another dimension to Jesus that is less popular and in a way almost unknown to those who may have grown up listening to Bible stories but have not searched the scriptures themselves. Our Master, who loved and loves with a depth and feels with a compassion that we cannot comprehend, also despised self-righteousness. The four Gospels frequently portray the Lord as condemning those who think they are in some way better than their fellows, those whose claim to righteousness is more pretense than reality.

Only days before his crucifixion, Jesus excoriated the pious ones: "Woe unto you, scribes and Pharisees, hypocrites!

for ye pay tithe of mint and anise and cummin, and have omitted the weightier matters of the law, judgment, mercy, and faith. . . . Ye blind guides, which strain [out] a gnat, and swallow a camel. Woe unto you, scribes and Pharisees, hypocrites! for ye make clean the outside of the cup and of the platter, but within they are full of extortion and excess. . . . Woe unto you, scribes and Pharisees, hypocrites! for ye are like unto whited sepulchres, which indeed appear beautiful outward, but are within full of dead men's bones, and of all uncleanness. Even so ye also outwardly appear righteous unto men, but within ye are full of hypocrisy and iniquity" (Matthew 23:23–25, 27–28). Or, as Luke records, "Woe unto you, scribes and Pharisees, hypocrites! for ye are as graves which appear not, and the men that walk over them are not aware of them" (Luke 11:44).

The fall of Adam was a universal fall, and its effect is universal: Each of us is born into a world of sin, and each of us is enticed toward that which is unholy. In the words of Isaiah, "All we like sheep have gone astray; we have turned every one to his own way" (Isaiah 53:6). Truly, "there is none righteous, no, not one: there is none that understandeth, there is none that seek after God. . . . For all have sinned, and come short of the glory of God" (Romans 3:10–11, 23). Thus, each of us, no matter our ancestry and no matter our social standing, is in need of help—of divine help—if we are to enjoy peace and happiness here and eternal reward hereafter. Every person who is born into this life is in need of redemption and deliverance.

Two episodes in the New Testament testify in particularly touching ways of the sobering reality of the Fall and of the joyful tidings of the Atonement. Each affirms our utter helplessness when we are left to our own resources and strength.

The first story takes place after Jesus' healing of the man born blind. Because the healed man refused to denounce Jesus before the Pharisees, the leaders of the Jews cast him out—that is, they excommunicated him from the synagogue and thus ostracized him from family and friends. In a tender scene, "Jesus heard that they had cast him out; and when he had found him, he said unto him, Dost thou believe on the Son of God? He answered and said, Who is he, Lord, that I might believe on him? And Jesus said unto him, Thou hast both seen him, and it is he that talketh with thee. And he said, Lord, I believe. And he worshipped him" (John 9:35–38).

John recorded: "And Jesus said, For judgment I am come into this world, that they which see not might see; and that they which see might be made blind. And some of the Pharisees which were with him heard these words, and said unto him, Are we blind also? Jesus said unto them, If ye were blind, ye should have no sin: but now ye say, We see; therefore your sin remaineth" (John 9:39–41). What a seemingly strange statement! We understand that the Savior came into the world to open the eyes of the blind, both spiritually and temporally, and that he came to bring light to a darkened world. But what did he mean by stating he had also come "that they which see might be made blind"?

The Lord taught us through Moroni: "And if men come unto me I will show unto them their weakness. I give unto men weakness that they may be humble; and my grace is sufficient for all men that humble themselves before me; for if they humble themselves before me, and have faith in me, then will I make weak things become strong unto them" (Ether 12:27).

That same Lord had spoken to the apostle Paul: "My grace is sufficient for thee: for my strength is made perfect in weakness. Most gladly therefore," Paul added, "will I rather glory in my infirmities, that the power of Christ may rest upon me" (2 Corinthians 12:9). Our Master is able to make us strong, each one of us, but only if we are willing to confess and acknowledge our plight, our weakness, and thus our need for him. We are able to see only as the Lord peels

And not many days after the younger son gathered all together,

and took his journey into a far country,

and there wasted his substance with riotous living.

away from our eyes the layers of sin and duplicity and self-assurance.

He who holds all things in his power is the same who stills the storms of the human heart with a healing touch. Indeed, as Elder Howard W. Hunter observed, "Whatever Jesus lays his hands upon lives. If Jesus lays his hands upon a marriage, it lives. If he is allowed to lay his hands on the family, it lives."[2] But we must be willing to open ourselves to his tender touch. "Jesus never met a disease he could not cure, a birth defect he could not reverse, a demon he could not exorcise. But he did meet skeptics he could not convince and sinners he could not convert. Forgiveness of sins requires an act of will on the receiver's part, and some who heard Jesus' strongest words about grace and forgiveness turned away unrepentant."[3]

The second story is one of Jesus' parables, that of the Pharisee and the publican. "And he spake this parable unto certain which trusted in themselves that they were righteous, and despised others: Two men went up into the temple to pray; the one a Pharisee, and the other a publican. The Pharisee stood and prayed thus with himself, God, I thank thee, that I am not as other men are, extortioners, unjust, adulterers, or even as this publican. I fast twice in the week, I give tithes of all that I possess. And the publican, standing afar off, would not lift up so much as his eyes unto heaven, but smote upon his breast, saying, God be merciful to me a sinner." Jesus summarized the matter: "I tell you, this man [the publican] went down to his house justified, rather than the other: for every one that exalteth himself shall be abased; and he that humbleth himself shall be exalted" (Luke 18:9–14).

The Pharisees were one of the major religious sects in the days of Jesus. They considered themselves to be the separated ones, a step above the other people of the land in their observance of religious practices and ritual. They believed fully in the Torah, their holy scriptures, and subscribed also to what became known as the "tradition of the elders" (Matthew 15:2), the commentary on the scripture by learned rabbis, which had been transmitted orally over the generations since the time of Moses.

The publicans, on the other hand, were among the most hated and despised of all people. They were tax collectors, employees of the Roman government, and as such were considered traitors to their own nation because of their complicity with the despised overlords. Frequently, they prospered by charging more than a fair price for taxes and keeping the difference (Luke 3:12–13).

The Pharisees "trusted in themselves that they were

righteous" (Luke 18:9). That is, they determined their own goodness, measured their own faithfulness according to the traditions of the elders, and thereby established their own eternal reward based on the degree to which they paid their tithes or offerings, observed the Sabbath, and kept themselves aloof from ritually unclean persons or circumstances. Jesus—who called a tax collector (Matthew) as one of his chosen disciples (Matthew 9:9)—taught that "there is none good but one, that is, God" (Matthew 19:17). God's standards of right and wrong are preeminent and paramount, not man's. Too often, in fact, people who are "ignorant of God's righteousness" go about seeking to "establish their own righteousness" (Romans 10:3). Such was the case in this story.

The Pharisee's words betray that he feels he does not really need God; his impressive deeds are sufficient to save him. For example, he states aloud that he fasts twice a week. The Pharisees fasted on Mondays and Thursdays between major feasts and festivals during the year. In addition, they were scrupulous in the payment of their tithes. The publican, on the other hand, knowing his many sins, acknowledging his lowly station before man and God, simply pleaded for mercy. A stark contrast, to be sure, but it is the sinful publican, not the pious Pharisee, who went home forgiven, cleansed, and declared righteous.

Self-promotion is antithetical to personal spiritual progress. The parable of the Pharisee and the publican is a condemnation of hypocrisy and self-righteousness. The striking irony in the message of this parable is that all of us fall short of the divine standard, all of us are in need of pardoning mercy. Truly, the recognition of our plight, of our spiritual bankruptcy without divine assistance, is the beginning of wisdom, the door that opens us to strength and power beyond our own.

"Christ said he came to call sinners to repentance to save them," Joseph Smith declared. "Christ was condemned by the self-righteous Jews because He took sinners into His society; He took them upon the principle that they repented of their sins. . . .

"Nothing is so calculated to lead people to forsake sin as to take them by the hand, and watch over them with tenderness. When persons manifest the least kindness and love to me, O what power it has over my mind, while the opposite course has a tendency to harrow up all the harsh feelings and depress the human mind.

"It is one evidence that men are unacquainted with the principles of godliness to behold the contraction of affectionate feelings and lack of charity in the world. The power and glory of godliness is spread out on a broad principle to throw out the mantle of charity. God does not look on sin with allowance, but when men have sinned, there must be allowance made for them.

"All the religious world is boasting of righteousness: it is the doctrine of the devil to retard the human mind, and hinder our progress, by filling us with self-righteousness. . . .

" . . . There should be no license for sin, but mercy should go hand in hand with reproof."[4]

One Christian writer has observed: "Jesus was 'the man for others.' . . . He kept himself free—free for the other person. He would accept almost anybody's invitation to dinner, and as a result no public figure had a more diverse list of friends, ranging from rich people, Roman centurions, and Pharisees to tax collectors, prostitutes, and leprosy victims. People *liked* being with Jesus; where he was, joy was."[5]

In that spirit, let us consider the introductory words of Luke 15, for these few verses set the stage and provide the interpretation for the parables that follow:

"Then drew near unto him all the publicans and sinners for to hear him. And the Pharisees and scribes murmured, saying, This man receiveth sinners, and eateth with them.

And he spake this parable unto them, saying . . ." (Luke 15:1–3).

That's it. That's the background. The Master is surrounded by people who are despised by the upper crust of society and the religious establishment, and the pious ones remark, essentially, "If this man really were divine, if he really were the promised Messiah, the Holy One of Israel, surely he would not be found in the midst of such disgusting folk." As one biblical scholar noted, "The term 'sinners' means: (1) People who led an immoral life (e.g. adulterers, swindlers, Luke 18:11) and (2) people who followed a dishonorable calling (i.e. an occupation which notoriously involved immorality or dishonesty), and who were on that account deprived of civil rights, such as holding office, or bearing witness in legal proceedings. For example, excise-men, tax collectors, shepherds, donkey-drivers, pedlars, and tanners."[6]

What was the problem with Jesus' eating with publicans and sinners? In ancient times, table fellowship was said to create a close bond between individuals. "The Pharisees themselves (as well as other Jewish groups) shared common meals as a major component of their group identity. All the more reason there was, then, to criticize Jesus for his action, which implied the creation of a social bond between him and his fellow table companions."[7]

Again we may turn to Joseph Smith, who had such pene-
trating insights into the nature of man, to better understand
the parables of Luke 15: "In reference to the prodigal son, I
said it was a subject I had never dwelt upon; that it was
understood by many to be one of the intricate subjects of the
scriptures; and even the Elders of this Church have preached
largely upon it, without having any rule of interpretation.
What is the rule of interpretation? Just no interpretation at
all. Understand it precisely as it reads. I have a key by which I
understand the scriptures. I enquire, what was the question
which drew out the answer, or caused Jesus to utter the parable? . . . To ascertain its meaning, we must dig up the root
and ascertain what it was that drew the saying out of Jesus.

"While Jesus was teaching the people, all the publicans
and sinners drew near to hear Him; 'and the Pharisees and
scribes murmured, saying: This man receiveth sinners, and
eateth with them.' This is the keyword which unlocks the
parable of the prodigal son. It was given to answer the mur-
murings and questions of the Sadducees and Pharisees, who
were querying, finding fault, and saying, 'How is it that this
man as great as He pretends to be, eats with publicans and
sinners?'"[8]

Let us consider briefly the first parable of Luke 15. "And
he spake this parable unto them, saying, What man of you,

having an hundred sheep, if he lose one of them, doth not leave the ninety and nine in the wilderness, and go after that which is lost, until he find it? And when he hath found it, he layeth it on his shoulders, rejoicing. And when he cometh home, he calleth together his friends and neighbours, saying unto them, Rejoice with me; for I have found my sheep which was lost. I say unto you, that likewise joy shall be in heaven over one sinner that repenteth, more than over ninety and nine just persons, which need no repentance" (Luke 15:3–7).

In this parable, a prized possession wanders off on its own in search of food. We do not suppose neglect on the part of the shepherd but rather distraction and inattention on the part of the foolish sheep. The one sheep is precious, worthy of extra effort, worthy of the risk of leaving the ninety and nine for a brief season. Besides, the ninety and nine "intact" ones are just as lost in their own way.

Joseph Smith explained: "The hundred sheep represent one hundred Sadducees and Pharisees, as though Jesus had said, 'If you Sadducees and Pharisees are in the sheepfold, I have no mission for you; I am sent to look up sheep that are lost; and when I have found them, I will back them up and make joy in heaven.' This represents hunting after a few individuals, or one poor publican, which the Pharisees and Sadducees despised."[9]

Indeed, when the Good Shepherd has found one that is lost, he lifts and lightens the burdens of the wanderer, takes the weight of sin upon his back, and leads the sheep back to safety within the household of faith. In like manner, those of us who are disciples of Christ are called as undershepherds, as apprentices to the merciful and forgiving One. Truly, "the nearer we get to our heavenly Father, the more we are disposed to look with compassion on perishing souls; we feel that we want to take them upon our shoulders, and cast their sins behind our backs."[10]

President David O. McKay asked: "How did that sheep get lost? He was not rebellious. If you follow the comparison, the lamb was seeking its livelihood in a perfectly legitimate manner, but either stupidly, perhaps unconsciously, it followed the enticement of the field, the prospect of better grass until it got out beyond the fold and was lost." President McKay then offered this application: "So we have those in the Church, young men and young women, who wander away from the fold in perfectly legitimate ways. They are seeking success, success in business, success in their professions, and before long they become disinterested in Church and finally disconnected from the fold; they have lost track of what true success is, perhaps stupidly, perhaps unconsciously, in some cases, perhaps willingly. They are blind to what constitutes true success."[11]

Now let us consider the second parable. "Either what woman having ten pieces of silver, if she lose one piece, doth not light a candle, and sweep the house, and seek diligently till she find it? And when she hath found it, she calleth her friends and her neighbours together, saying, Rejoice with me; for I have found the piece which I had lost. Likewise, I say unto you, there is joy in the presence of the angels of God over one sinner that repenteth" (Luke 15:8–10).

Here a precious item is lost because of the neglect of the owner. The Greek *drachma* was a silver coin of approximately the same value as the Roman *denarius;* it was worth about a day's wage. This too is a parable of chastisement, an accusation against those who see themselves as perpetually faithful. "There is joy in the presence of the angels of God," Joseph Smith stated, "over one sinner that repenteth, more than over ninety-and-nine just persons that are so righteous; they [the prideful ones] will be damned anyhow; you cannot save them."[12]

In the parable, the woman's heart seems to be right, her motives pure, her desire to retrieve that which is lost genuine. It certainly isn't something she planned to do; unfortunately, the coin was misplaced. In the same way, a brother or sister may be lost through our neglect: perhaps we weren't regular or consistent in our visits; perhaps we weren't as loving and welcoming as we might have been when he or she came to church; perhaps we weren't as willing to forgive and forget as we should have been. Perhaps the person was too eager to be hurt, too quick to take offense, too open to bruising by an ecclesiastical elbow. Whatever the cause, the under-shepherds search and watch and reach out in earnest antici-pation that the wandering one may be found. And the angels—including loved ones on both sides of the veil—exult in the reunion.

President McKay said further: "The second parable is the parable of the lost coin. A woman lost it, and, looking in vain to find it, called in the neighbors to help her search for it.

"In this case the thing lost was not in itself responsible. The one who had been trusted with that coin had, through carelessness or neglect, mislaid it or dropped it. There is a difference. Our charge is not only coins, but also living souls of children, youth, and adults. They are our charges. Some of them may be wandering tonight because of the neglect of the ward teachers whose duty it is to ' . . . watch over the church always, and be with and strengthen them. . . .

"Someone may be wandering because of the careless

remark of a girl of her age in Mutual. . . . Another may be lost because of the inactivity of the Sunday School teacher or the indifference of the Sunday School teacher who is satisfied with the fifteen people there that morning, instead of thinking of the fifteen who are wandering because of neglect.

"Our responsibility is to keep the trust that God has reposed in us, calling us to guard these precious souls."[13]

All that we have said leads us now to a deeper consideration of the third parable. In many ways, the parable of the prodigal son is the parable of parables. It distils the plan of life and salvation: It teaches of the purpose of life, the reality of the Fall and the challenges of this second estate, and the opportunity for redemption and renewal through the matchless love of God our Father and his precious Son, Jesus Christ. And it does all of this in a brief but poignant story—in twenty-two verses, to be exact.

This timeless classic reminds us (and oh, how we regularly need such reminders) how readily mortals are prone to wander; how eager a darkened and benighted world is to quench the light of truth and veil the memory of where we came from and who we really are; how painful but necessary it is to acknowledge our plight and see things as they really are; how easy it is for those who count themselves as worthy, at least by men's myopic standards, to judge unrighteously, to condemn, and to exclude from fellowship the wanderer who comes to himself; and, perhaps, most fundamental, how warm and welcoming is the embrace of God, of a waiting Father whose love is incomparable, never ending, and thus soul transforming.

Luke gives us these three parables about lost things—a lost sheep, a lost coin, and a lost son—three brief stories that emphasize how easy it is for human souls to stray in ignorance, be lost through neglect, and, most painfully, wander through conscious choice. And yet these three simple testimonies of the Master foster a consummate hope, a more excellent hope in the promise of divine forgiveness and the possibility of returning home. Truly, our hearts cry out to our Maker:

> O to grace how great a debtor
> Daily I'm constrained to be!
> Let thy goodness, as a fetter,
> Bind my wandering heart to thee.
>
> Prone to wander, Lord, I feel it,
> Prone to leave the God I love;
> Here's my heart, O take and seal it;
> Seal it for thy courts above.[14]

PART TWO

And when he had spent all, there arose a mighty famine

in that land; and he began to be in want. And he went

and joined himself to a citizen of that country;

and he sent him into his fields to feed swine. And he

would fain have filled his belly with the husks

that the swine did eat; and no man gave unto him.

The Parable and Commentary

The parable of the prodigal son, a beautiful and elevating story in any translation of the New Testament, is in the language of the King James Version particularly moving. Although some biblical scholars may claim greater clarity through more modern translations, the words of the King James Version are touching and memorable. Such phrases as the following have warmed the human heart for centuries; they are, in fact, unforgettable: "a far country"; "wasted his substance with riotous living"; "when he came to himself"; "I will arise and go to my father"; "bring hither the fatted calf"; "Son, thou art ever with me, and all that I have is thine"; "this thy brother was . . . lost, and is found."

A certain man had two sons:

And the younger of them said to his father, Father, give me the portion of goods that falleth to me. And he divided unto them his living.

And not many days after the younger son gathered all together, and took his journey into a far country, and there wasted his substance with riotous living.

And when he had spent all, there arose a mighty famine in that land; and he began to be in want.

And he went and joined himself to a citizen of that country; and he sent him into his fields to feed swine.

And he would fain have filled his belly with the husks that the swine did eat: and no man gave unto him.

And when he came to himself, he said, How many hired servants of my father's have bread enough and to spare, and I perish with hunger!

I will arise and go to my father, and will say unto him, Father, I have sinned against heaven, and before thee,

And am no more worthy to be called thy son: make me as one of thy hired servants.

And he arose, and came to his father. But when he was yet

a great way off, his father saw him, and had compassion, and ran, and fell on his neck, and kissed him.

And the son said unto him, Father, I have sinned against heaven, and in thy sight, and am no more worthy to be called thy son.

But the father said to his servants, Bring forth the best robe, and put it on him; and put a ring on his hand, and shoes on his feet:

And bring hither the fatted calf, and kill it; and let us eat, and be merry:

For this my son was dead, and is alive again; he was lost, and is found. And they began to be merry.

Now his elder son was in the field: and as he came and drew nigh to the house, he heard musick and dancing.

And he called one of the servants, and asked what these things meant.

And he said unto him, Thy brother is come; and thy father hath killed the fatted calf, because he hath received him safe and sound.

And he was angry, and would not go in: therefore came his father out, and intreated him.

And he answering said to his father, Lo, these many years do I serve thee, neither transgressed I at any time thy

commandment: and yet thou never gavest me a kid, that I
might make merry with my friends:

But as soon as this thy son was come, which hath devoured
thy living with harlots, thou hast killed for him the fatted calf.

And he said unto him, Son, thou art ever with me, and all
that I have is thine.

It was meet that we should make merry, and be glad: for
this thy brother was dead, and is alive again; and was lost, and
is found.

LUKE 15:11–32

Let us take the words of this remarkable parable a phrase
at a time, briefly commenting upon the verses of what many
believe to be the greatest of all parables.

11. And he said, A certain man had two sons:

The parable of the prodigal son may be divided into two
parts, almost two parables: Verses 11 through 24 deal with
the younger son, and verses 25 through 32 deal with the
older son.

12. And the younger of them said to his father, Father, give
me the portion of goods that falleth to me. And he divided unto
them his living.

The younger son seems to have wanted his "freedom." President David O. McKay noted that the younger son "was immature in his judgment. He was irking under the restraint, and he rather resented the father's careful, guiding eye. He evidently longed for so-called freedom, wanted, so to speak, to try his wings. . . .

"Here is a case of volition, here is choice, deliberate choice. Here is, in a way, rebellion against authority."[1]

The situation between the younger son and his father has been described by one writer in terms that are especially helpful to us today:

"Surely the father and son in the parable must have talked about this many times. The son would say, 'Father, I want to be independent. You must give me my freedom. I can't go on listening to this everlasting "Thou shalt" and "Thou shalt not."' And the father replies: 'My dear boy, do you really think you have no freedom? After all, you are the child in the house, you can come to me any time you wish, and you can tell me anything and everything that troubles you. Many a person would be happy to have such a son's privilege. Isn't that freedom? Look, my whole kingdom belongs to you. . . .'

"And the son flares up and says, 'No, father, to be honest with you, I don't care a hoot about all that. I can't stand this constant training. For me freedom means to be able to do what I want to do.' And the father quietly replies, 'And for me freedom means that you should become what you ought to be. . . . *That's* why I forbid you so many things. Not to limit your freedom but just the opposite, in order that you may remain free of all this, that you may become worthy of your origin and be free for sonship. . . .'

"But the son leaves the room grumbling and slams the door. Naturally, he knows that the father is right. But he can't use this rightness now. He has other plans and what his father says does not suit him now; it does not fit with the way *he* wants to live. It is too terribly narrow for him. . . .

"The son has a dreadful fear that he will not taste life to the full, that he may miss something. 'Is that bad?' he asks himself (for he is not a bad fellow at heart). He feels a tremendous urge to live and he is ready to fight for it and carry it out. . . .

" . . . 'I want all this just *once;* then I'll come back. Just *once* let my body have its fling, *one* ecstasy. After all, you must be able to do that *too,* otherwise a fellow is not a "real man" and never develops his full potential. Then I'll come back!' "[2]

The younger son—we suppose he was unmarried and thus somewhere between seventeen and twenty years of age—went to the father and asked that the property, presumably the land, be divided up. Under Jewish law a father could not leave his property to whomever he wanted. He was required to leave a double portion to the elder son, so in this case two-thirds would be left to the elder son and one-third to the younger (Deuteronomy 21:17). But the division was not generally done until the father's death. The younger son was essentially saying to the father, "Look, I'll get this share when you die anyway. Give it to me now."

"What is happening here is an unheard-of event; hurtful, offensive, and in radical contradiction to the most venerated tradition of the time," one Roman Catholic writer explained.[3] A researcher who lived in the Near East for many years observed: "For over fifteen years I have been asking people of all walks of life from Morocco to India and from Turkey to the Sudan about the implications of a son's request for his inheritance while the father is still living. The answer has almost always been emphatically the same.... The conversation runs as follows:

"Has anyone ever made such a request in your village?

"Never!

"Could anyone ever make such a request?

"Impossible!

"If anyone ever did, what would happen?

"His father would beat him, of course!

"Why?

"The request means—he wants his father to die."[4]

"The son's 'leaving' is, therefore, a much more offensive act than it seems at first reading. It is a heartless rejection of the home in which the son was born and nurtured and a break with the most precious tradition carefully upheld by the larger community of which he was a part."[5]

In allotting to the younger son his one-third, the father was thereby formally allotting to the elder son his two-thirds, but this action does not necessarily mean that he gave the elder son his portion then. The father was still in charge thereafter: He commanded the servants (v. 22), ordered the slaughter of the fatted calf (v. 23), and spoke of "all that I have" (v. 31).

Why would the father do this? Why would he "enable" the younger son? Perhaps he wanted the boy to learn, through life's hard lessons, that freedom and happiness cannot be had without God.

13. And not many days after the younger son gathered all together, and took his journey into a far country, and there wasted his substance with riotous living.

Probably the younger son sold the land and converted his inheritance into cash, something he was certainly within his legal rights to do but something that stretched the moral law. Given the importance of land and of how, no doubt, the land was linked to the family, such a move would have been very painful and embarrassing for the family and even scandalous to the community.

Of the prodigal son's break with the family, one writer declared: "The younger son's breach with the family was total. He gathered '*all* he had,' traveled to a *distant* country'; no property of his should remain with them [the family], because as long as what belongs to him is with them, he is, in a sense, with them and they are with him. And in the distant country he did exactly the opposite of what a member of a good household should do: he '*squandered*' the inheritance in '*dissolute* living.' (v. 13). All behavioral patterns learned at home must be put aside, because as long as he behaves like a son he is a son, and home is with him and he is, in a sense, at home. His project was to 'un-son' himself; there was no place in him for the place called home. That the father considered him 'lost,' even 'dead' (v. 24) confirms this. Departure was not an act of separation required for the formation of a distinct identity, but an act of exclusion by which the self pulls itself out of the relationships without which it would not be what it is, and cuts itself off from responsibilities to others and makes itself their enemy."[6]

No doubt the young man traveled into the Diaspora, into a Gentile land to which Jews had been scattered. The size of the Diaspora in the first century has been estimated at more than four million; the number of Jews in Palestine was half a million at the most.

How typical of our second estate, our life on earth, is the notion that the younger son "took his journey into a far country." At birth we leave the safety and security of life with our Heavenly Parents, leave behind that knowledge and those associations that had been developed over eons of time, separate ourselves from the experience and understanding that make us who we were and are. Indeed, as we sing in the beloved hymn, our Father has

> withheld the recollection
> Of my former friends and birth;
> Yet ofttimes a secret something
> Whispered "You're a stranger here,"
> And I felt that I had wandered
> From a more exalted sphere.[7]

At some point, the wisest among us confess that we are strangers and pilgrims on the earth (Hebrews 11:13), that we are only visitors in this temporary tenement, that we have indeed "wandered from a more exalted sphere." And the great question facing each of us is whether we will attune our souls and be loyal to what we have been taught, to what we know deep within us to be true.

"Like the prodigal son," Elder Neal A. Maxwell taught, "we too can go to 'a far country,' which may be no farther away than a vile rock concert. The distance to 'a far country' is not to be measured by miles but by how far our hearts and minds are from Jesus! (see Mosiah 5:13). Fidelity, not geography, really determines the distance!"[8]

We are not told what the young man's sins were, only that he seems to have spent his inheritance quickly and frivolously. He surely had "friends" who were eager to help him spend his money but who disappeared quite suddenly when the funds were gone and the fun was over.

14. And when he had spent all, there arose a mighty famine in that land; and he began to be in want.

Added to the problem of poverty is the challenge of a famine. In a famine there is no food—people are starving. That is, not only did the prodigal run out of money but he also had to reckon with an economic crisis. We do not notice a famine as much when we have money, but we really feel it when we're broke. Here he is, a Jew, alone in an alien nation, and outsiders inevitably acquire the worst jobs with the lowest pay.

15. And he went and joined himself to a citizen of that country; and he sent him into his fields to feed swine.

The young man attached himself to a man who was a citizen of that far country. Given his personal financial straits and also the economic condition of the country, any job, anything that would keep body and spirit together, looked good at that moment.

The son took a job as a pig feeder, a task that was counter to all he had been taught. "At this point his status is that of an indentured servant—a status above that of a slave, but one that bound him by contract to work as a general laborer for his employer for a specified time. To feed pigs is degradation of the worst sort. Pigs are unclean animals in law and tradition (Lev. 11:7; Deut. 14:8; cf. Isaiah 65:4; 66:17; 1 Macc. 1:47; cf. 2 Macc. 6:18; 7:1). According to the *Mishnah,* from subsequent centuries, no one is allowed to rear swine, and according to the *Babylonian Talmud,* the person who does so is accursed."[9] Truly, feeding swine was as low as a young Jewish man could descend.

16. And he would fain have filled his belly with the husks that the swine did eat: and no man gave unto him.

The prodigal was starving and would have eaten the feed of animals. In a sense, "the very idea of wishing to be fed from the 'pods' eaten by pigs—and therefore being envious of the pigs!—but being refused, is even more degrading than the act of feeding the pigs itself."[10]

Why did he not eat the "husks"? Some scholars suggest that he was utterly disgusted at the depths to which he had sunk and refused to eat animal food. Others state that verse 16 implies he would gladly have eaten the husks but the people in charge would not give him any. If the latter explanation is true, it is tragically the case that he was considered less than the pigs. Let's be frank here. Which is worth more in a famine—pigs or poor people? Clearly, pigs. Pigs bring in money; poor people bring in nothing. The people in charge thus do not want to waste good pig feed on a poor Jewish lad.

How free is the young man now? He is not free from hunger, from sorrow, from emptiness and alienation. He is at the bottom. Truly, there are some hungers that cannot be satisfied, some sorrows that cannot be handled, apart from God.

17. And when he came to himself, he said, How many hired servants of my father's have bread enough and to spare, and I perish with hunger!

When he woke up, came alive, and realized his plight, he

saw himself as he was. Henri Nouwen observed: "I see before me a man who went deep into a foreign land and lost everything he took with him. I see emptiness, humiliation, and defeat. He who was so much like his father now looks worse than his father's servants. He has become like a slave.

"What happened to the son in the distant country? Aside from all the material and physical consequences, what were the inner consequences of the son's leaving home? The sequence of events is quite predictable. The farther I run away from the place where God dwells, the less I am able to hear the voice that calls me the Beloved, and the less I hear that voice, the more entangled I become in the manipulations and power games of the world. . . .

"The younger son became fully aware of how lost he was when no one in his surroundings showed the slightest interest in him. They noticed him only as long as he could be used for their purposes. But when he had no money left to spend and no gifts left to give, he stopped existing for them. It is hard for me to imagine what it means to be a complete foreigner, a person to whom no one shows any sign of recognition. Real loneliness comes when we have lost all sense of having things in common. When no one wanted to give him the food he was giving to the pigs, the younger son realized that he wasn't even considered a fellow human being."[11]

Does his conscience bring him to himself, or is it his hunger? It is probably his hunger—which includes his feelings of alienation and loss—that activates his memory. When the wanderer comes to himself, "he remembers the other whom he wanted to push out of his world but to whom he found himself still belonging. . . . Through departure he wanted to become a 'non-son'; his return begins not with repentance but with something that makes the repentance possible—the memory of sonship. *There is no coming to oneself without the memory of belonging.* The self has been constructed in relation to others, and it can come to itself only through relationship to others. The first link with the other in a distant country of broken relationships is memory." In short, "for him whose project was to 'un-son' himself and who is still in a distant country, 'sonship' can only be a memory, but it is a memory that defines his present so much that it sets him on a journey back. The memory of sonship gives hope."[12]

It has been observed that "the beginning of wisdom is to come to our senses and know the fearful truth about ourselves, that we have wandered and wasted our days in a distant country far from home."[13]

The prodigal son was in much the same condition as the Zoramites in the Book of Mormon: They were "compelled to be humble" (Alma 32:13). But being compelled to be humble is not all bad, for it often places us in "a preparation to hear the word" (Alma 32:6).

"And now," Alma pointed out, "because ye are compelled to be humble blessed are ye; for a man sometimes, if he is compelled to be humble, seeketh repentance; and now surely, whosoever repenteth shall find mercy; and he that findeth mercy and endureth to the end the same shall be saved" (Alma 32:13).

Elder Neal A. Maxwell stated that "the returning prodigals are never numerous enough, but regularly some come back from 'a far country' (Luke 15:13). Of course, it is better if we are humbled 'because of the word' rather than being compelled by circumstances, yet the latter may do! (See Alma 32:13–14). Famine can induce spiritual hunger."[14]

18–19. I will arise and go to my father, and will say unto him, Father, I have sinned against heaven, and before thee, and am no more worthy to be called thy son: make me as one of thy hired servants.

It is not easy to arise, to repent, to "turn away" or "turn about" (Hebrew meaning), to open oneself to a "change of mind" or seek for a "higher way of thinking" (Greek meaning). In fact, it takes a great deal of personal effort, coupled with divine strength, to choose to be changed, to work against the spiritual inertia so common in our fallen world. Repentance is not just a human work, not something we do completely on our own (Acts 5:29–31; 11:18; 2 Timothy 2:23–25; Alma 34:14–15). In fact, "godly sorrow is a gift of the Spirit."[15]

Once wanderers hit bottom, particularly wanderers who were taught better and have lived for a time in the light, it is fairly common for them to come to themselves. They realize what they once had, and they recognize the famine for the word of truth in their own lives in the present emptiness of their souls. Deep within their hearts, they begin to long for the sweet peace they once knew. Those who view themselves "in their own carnal state, even less than the dust of the earth" (Mosiah 4:2), feel the need to confess their sins and acknowledge their spiritual bankruptcy before God.

And what should the prodigal son expect from his father? From the community? Ridicule, rejection, verbal and perhaps even physical abuse? Surely during those agonizing moments of introspection and personal confrontation, the wanderer must have reflected on what a return trip would mean. Surely he must have realized that the "righteous ones" in the community would demand that every ounce of justice be administered in as painful and humiliating a way as possible.

How had the prodigal sinned against heaven (God) and against his father? He had broken the commandments of God set forth in the law of Moses. For one thing, he had failed to honor his father and mother (Exodus 20:12) and had brought heartbreak and anxiety and embarrassment to the whole family. He had humiliated his father in the community and had caused him grief.

The prodigal had sinned against the family and forfeited, according to traditional Jewish thinking, his right to be a member of his father's family. He had excluded himself from the blessings of the covenant. In tending swine, he had violated the law of Moses and its standards of ritual purity; a Jew by birth and training, he had lived the life of the Gentile. "The youth is morally unfit to be regarded as a son, whether or not he has been legally disowned. He has no claims on his father after the earlier settlement of his portion, and can only ask to be given the position of a servant in a household where servants are known to be well-treated."[16]

Beseeching his father to make him as one of the "hired servants," the prodigal was asking to be taken into the household as one of the very least of its members. Of the three kinds of servants in Israel at the time of Jesus, the highest

And when he came to himself, he said, How many

hired servants of my father's have bread enough and to spare,

and I perish with hunger! I will arise and go to my father,

and will say unto him, Father,

I have sinned against heaven,

and before thee, and am no more

worthy to be called thy son;

make me as one of thy

hired servants.

ranking were the bondsmen. Although they were slaves, they were part of the estate and practically members of the family. Below them were the lower-class servants, also slaves, who were subordinate to the bondsmen. Their lives were harder, but they were to a lesser degree part of the estate and the family. Lowest of all were the "hired servants"—day laborers, temporary workers, outsiders—who did not belong to the estate or the family and who might, without notice, be dismissed; they often lived in destitute conditions.

20. And he arose, and came to his father. But when he was yet a great way off, his father saw him, and had compassion, and ran, and fell on his neck, and kissed him.

It is worth noting that the son came, not to the estate, not to the house, but to his father. He knew where he needed to go. He knew where he needed to begin. That the young man indicated his intention to "go to my father" suggests strongly the father's loving, understanding, and forgiving disposition, a man who would stand firmly for righteousness, to be sure, but whose compassion would make a repenting son feel that he could safely return.

Clearly, the father has been looking for his son for a long time, regularly and consistently going to the window, waiting, waiting for any word at all. Although the faithful parents of a wanderer need not be preoccupied or consumed with worry nor be dysfunctional in their fears and grief, still, every time the phone rings, every time a car approaches, hope springs up in their hearts.

It would not be unusual for parents to have hardened themselves to the wanderer, developing an attitude of "Show me" or "Prove yourself" or "Let's don't rush into this." The mother and father might have concluded, "Let's not make a big fuss over him, because right now we just don't know what to make of his return." There might have been too many emotional roller-coaster rides, too many tears, too many dashed hopes, too much pain for a reasonable parent to take any other attitude.

"Even though the father has compassion on his son, a proper response for him would be to let the young man arrive home, fall on his knees, and ask for forgiveness. Then, in the best of all circumstances, the father would respond with words of forgiveness and a review of expectations. The son would, in effect, be on probation around home for a time; perhaps he could remain there until he could earn enough to leave as an independent person once again."[17]

Instead, the account simply states, the father "had compassion."

In the Near East, for an elderly gentleman to run was

disgraceful. He often had long, flowing robes, and running would require him to roll up his robes, allowing people to see his naked legs. That would be humiliating; it would be "out-landish behavior."[18]

Kenneth Bailey wrote: "The father is fully aware of how his son will be treated, if and when he returns in humiliation to the village community he has rejected. What the father does in this homecoming scene can best be understood as a series of dramatic actions calculated to protect the boy from the hostility of the village and to restore him to fellowship within the community. These actions begin with the father running down the road.

"An Oriental nobleman with flowing robes never runs anywhere. To do so is humiliating. . . . The text says, 'He had compassion.' We would suggest that this 'compassion' specifi-cally includes awareness of the gauntlet the boy will have to face as he makes his way through the village. The father then runs this gauntlet for him, assuming a humiliating posture in the process!

"The father makes the reconciliation public at the edge of the village. Thus his son enters the village under the pro-tective care of the father's acceptance. The boy, having steeled his nerves for this gauntlet, now, to his utter amazement, sees his father run it for him. Rather than experiencing the ruthless hostility he deserves and anticipates, the son witnesses an unexpected, visible demonstration of love in humiliation. The father's acts replace speech. There are no words of acceptance and welcome. The love expressed is too profound for words. Only acts will do."[19]

Why did the father run? Because he was overjoyed to see his son. Because he had feared that his beloved son was dead. Because he was filled with love and compassion. Because he was eager to welcome home his son. These are the obvious reasons. Less obvious is that in heaping embarrassment and even humiliation upon himself by running to meet this prodigal son, the father was accepting the brunt of the community's scorn and ridicule. Bailey reports that a man in the modern Near East, an acquaintance of his, was rejected as a pastor by the elders of the city because he walked down the street too quickly![20]

When the father reached his son, he smothered him with kisses. Some of the rabbis of the time might have been incensed at this action. They would have felt that until the young man had washed himself thoroughly and thus made himself ritually clean, the father should not touch him. This display by the father was not a formal reception but a very visible example of forgiveness and welcome. How would these actions make the son feel? They were a silent sermon.

The father's kiss was "a sign of reconciliation and forgiveness. When a serious quarrel has taken place in the village and reconciliation is achieved, a part of the ceremony enacted as a sacrament of reconciliation is a public kiss by the leading men involved."[21]

21. And the son said unto him, Father, I have sinned against heaven, and in thy sight, and am no more worthy to be called thy son.

We note that the returning prodigal altered his prepared speech: he left out the part he had planned to say about becoming a hired servant. Does this reveal something about him that is sinister and conniving? Has the overly warm welcome caused him to rethink things and say to himself, "Hey, wait a minute. Let's don't sell ourselves short here!"

Although that certainly might be the case with some wanderers, the parable suggests otherwise. The display of pure love on the part of the father seems to have made the son's planned speech inappropriate. Whereas the prodigal's anticipated apology and proposal would have put him into a bargaining and negotiating posture (in an attitude of "give me some time, and I'll pay you back what I owe you"), the love of the father has melted all that away.

The young man's leaving home in the way that he did

damaged a relationship. And we do not repair relationships with money. "As soon as the son says that he is no longer worthy to be called a son of his father, the father has heard more than enough. His response is to treat him as more than a son. He is a special guest!"[22]

As Elder Bruce R. McConkie wrote: "The father, who yet loved his wayward son, was waiting, hoping, praying for his return. He has a fatted calf in the stall for a planned feast; now he sees the erring one a great way off, hastens to him, and greets him with tender compassion. The son confesses his sins—without which forgiveness cannot come—and because he has been so graciously received as a son, he does not make the contemplated offer to serve in a menial capacity as a hired servant. The two of them return to the home."[23]

22. But the father said to his servants, Bring forth the best robe, and put it on him; and put a ring on his hand, and shoes on his feet:

What the father does here is crucial. Why didn't he simply hug his son and say, "Well, go on inside, son, and we'll discuss it later"? That would have said something about the young man—that he was contemptible, that he was not to be received back as a son. The people in the community probably expected the father, if he accepted the prodigal back at all, to disinherit him, at best to consign him to a slave's quarters and slave's food. But what the father said to the servants was, essentially, "Accept him as your master."

The father called for "the best robe," literally, the first robe, the finest robe, the foremost robe, the finest piece of clothing in the house, the robe worn by the master or distinguished guests on festive occasions. Similarly, Rebekah had given a special robe to Jacob (Genesis 27:15), and Pharaoh had presented one to Joseph (Genesis 41:42).

Then the father's ring, his signet ring, was placed on the prodigal's hand. It gave the bearer access to the estate's most important documents and possessions. "Excavations have shown that the ring is to be regarded as a signet-ring; the gift of a ring signified the bestowal of authority."[24] The ring was "not simply an ornament, but a symbol of authority, especially of royal authority."[25]

Slaves went barefoot, but free men wore shoes. With shoes on his feet, the young man returned to prestige. Further, the servants are asked to place the shoes on the prodigal, thus suggesting his reinstatement as a member of the family. The shoes "were worn in the house by the master, and not by the guests, who took them off on arrival. Hence they indicated authority and possession as well as freedom."[26]

23. And bring hither the fatted calf, and kill it; and let us eat, and be merry:

The father called for the grain-fed animal. Although most of the cattle grazed on grass, the animal designated for festive occasions was fed grain to cause it to put on extra weight and make its flesh more tender. It was a great tribute to have a fatted calf slaughtered in one's honor. An animal such as this might feed a hundred people, so it is clear that the banquet for the prodigal stretched beyond the family to the community. "Meat, which is rarely eaten, marks this as a special occasion."[27]

24. For this my son was dead, and is alive again; he was lost, and is found. And they began to be merry.

Lehi "spake concerning the prophets, how great a number had testified . . . concerning this Messiah, of whom he had spoken, or this Redeemer of the world. Wherefore, all mankind were in a lost and in a fallen state, and ever would be save they should rely on this Redeemer" (1 Nephi 10:5–6). Without the Lord we are lost; we cannot find the way save we should look to him who is the Way (John 14:6). Out in the desert we wander, hungry and helpless and cold; but off to the rescue the Good Shepherd hastens, bringing us back to the fold.[28]

Because of the Fall, all men and women are subject to spiritual death—separation between man and God, separation between us and things of righteousness (2 Nephi 2:21; Ether 3:2). Without the redemption of our Savior and the ordinances of salvation, we would remain forever lost and fallen; we would remain natural men and women. In our natural or unregenerated state, we are lost and spiritually dead; only in and through Christ are we found and spiritually resuscitated. Jesus is our only hope; he has been sent by the Father on a search-and-rescue mission to the wayward sheep: his is the offer to bind up our wounds and provide warmth and comfort and security through life within his sheepfold. President Joseph F. Smith pointed out that the prodigal son "had been dead to virtue, truth and honor, he had come to life again, so far as he could; and though he had been lost to reason, to common sense, and even to hope, he was found again, and hope was again revived for him. These were the reasons for rejoicing."[29]

It would be perfectly satisfying to most readers for the parable to end at this point, for a family seems to have been reunited with their wandering loved one. But the Savior did not choose to finish the story here, for the interpretation of this parable is tied to a different kind of problem.

And he arose, and came to his father. But when he was yet

a great way off, his father saw him, and had compassion,

and ran, and fell on his neck, and kissed him.

25–27. Now his elder son was in the field: and as he came and drew nigh to the house, he heard musick and dancing. And he called one of the servants, and asked what these things meant. And he [the servant] said unto him, Thy brother is come; and thy father hath killed the fatted calf, because he hath received him safe and sound.

The elder son was busy in the field; clearly, he is a hard worker, a devoted son. He has stayed home, been dutiful, and truly "earned" his portion of the inheritance. We are not told how far from the house the elder son has been working. For all we know, he may not have been near enough to have been informed about his brother's return. It seems strange that the father would not have spread the word far and wide, especially to family members, about the prodigal's return and the planned banquet. At any rate, lacking the details (for this is a parable, not really a short story), we find that the elder brother learns of the return and the celebration from a servant. One perspective indicates that "there are good reasons for not notifying him. Doubtless the father knows that the older brother will be upset and, if notified, may even try to prevent the banquet."[30]

We must never denigrate in any way the elder son's steadiness and faithfulness to the rules of the household. It is, to be sure, the elder sons of this world who get the work done, move things forward, maintain stability in society. But that is not what this parable is about. Like the Pharisees who complain of Jesus' acceptance of the publicans and sinners, the elder brother here complained of the father's acceptance of a sinful son. In a sense, the elder son is the good son with the bad heart; even when the prodigal returns, the elder son is not yet home but is still lost.

28. And he was angry, and would not go in: therefore came his father out, and intreated him.

Why was he angry? One writer has suggested that "he is angry because some basic rules have been broken—not oppressive rules that destroy life, but rules without which no civil life would be possible. The one who works (v. 29) deserves more recognition than the one who squanders; celebrating the squanderer is squandering. The one who obeys where obedience is due (v. 29) deserves more honor than the one who irresponsibly breaks commands; honoring the irresponsible is irresponsible. The one who remains faithful should be treated better than the one who excludes the others; preference for the excluding one is tacit exclusion of the faithful one. When squandering becomes better than working and the breach of relationships better than faithfulness, justice will be perverted and the household will fall apart."[31]

In short, the father's attitudes and actions were foreign to the cultural canons of right-wrong, good-bad, reward-punishment, typical rules by which we operate in a world like ours.

Moses had decreed anciently: "If a man have a stubborn and rebellious son, which will not obey the voice of his father, or the voice of his mother, and that, when they have chastened him, will not hearken unto them: then shall his father and his mother lay hold on him, and bring him out unto the elders of his city, and unto the gate of his place; and they shall say unto the elders of his city, This our son is stubborn and rebellious, he will not obey our voice; he is a glutton, and a drunkard. And all the men of his city shall stone him with stones, that he die: so shalt thou put evil away from among you; and all Israel shall hear, and fear" (Deuteronomy 21:18–21).

Surely the elder brother, even in his worst moments of anger, would not have desired this full measure of justice for his wandering brother. But it all seemed so very unfair to him.

"The shock of this public action [the elder son's refusing to go inside] is beyond description. The equivalent in Western society might be some case of a wealthy leading figure in a Western community who has a candlelight formal banquet for his most important friends and associates. In the middle of the banquet his unshaven son appears without a shirt or shoes and verbally attacks his father in the presence of the seated guests. Such a scene would be excruciatingly painful for the father. It would show *utter* disregard for the feelings and personal dignity of that father on the part of his son."[32]

Further, "at such a banquet the older son has a special semi-official responsibility. He is expected to move among the guests, offering compliments, making sure everyone has enough to eat, ordering the servants around and, in general, becoming a sort of major-domo of the feast."[33]

"The father, risking humiliation and shame, leaves his guests inside the house, goes outdoors, and pleads with the elder son to come in and join the celebration."[34] We might be inclined to say to the father, "Let the older son stew in his juices. He needs to grow up, show some love, and be the man he should be. Let him stay out in the field; he can miss the fun." But the father's tender regard for both of his children is evident; he cannot be completely happy while one of his sons is unhappy, festering in anger, or missing out on the opportunity to rejoice with the rest of the household.

President Joseph F. Smith commented on the father's entreaty to his elder son: "Now we may suppose the father

reasoned with him somewhat in this wise: 'My son, I am sur-
prised at your short sightedness; you should not be jealous
of your poor, unfortunate brother, for he is to be pitied; he
has squandered his substance, and I thought he was lost forever, that he was as good as dead to me, and hope for his
restoration to us had fled. But he has returned in sorrow for
his follies, in abject poverty, penitent and humble, freely con-
fessing that he has sinned against heaven and in my sight,
and that he is unworthy to be my son or your brother, and
would become our servant forever. Shall we not have compassion upon him, shall we utterly banish him from us, since
he has returned so humble and repentant? I love him as my
son, but with my love for him is mingled sorrow, pity, cha-
grin and commiseration. You have been faithful to me all the
while, and in you I have exceeding great joy. I love you with
all the affection of my soul, and in you I have perfect confi-
dence, for you have never betrayed it. Beside all this, you have
forfeited nothing nor lost anything. . . . Can we not well
afford to be charitable and forgiving?"[35]

*29. And he answering said to his father, Lo, these many
years do I serve thee, neither transgressed I at any time thy
commandment:*

Note the contempt in the elder brother's language; in his

choice of words he declares himself a slave of his father. He says not "my brother" but rather "this thy son" (meaning, "this son of yours").

The older brother's emotional distance signals his spiritual distance. In some ways, the hardest conversion is for the brother who chose to stay home. Maybe this story should be called the parable of the prodigal son*s*, for while the younger brother was lost to more visible sins, the older brother was lost in pride, self-righteousness, judgment, and resentment. Joy and resentment cannot coexist.

"It has been said and said truly, that the greatest fault is to be conscious of no fault. Self-righteousness shuts a man off both from God and men."[36] The excellent film *The Prodigal Son,* produced by the Church,[37] has a scene in which the elder, faithful brother and his wife are cleaning up after the party his father has hosted for the returning younger brother. The elder brother has made some very disparaging comments to his younger brother. Jim, the elder brother, asks his wife, "Why are you so quiet?"

"Because I'm not talking to you for a while," she responds.

"What did I do? Oh, I didn't fall all over my brother and kiss his feet, like everyone else. 'Oh, you're so wonderful, Tom. You're so great, Tom. It's so good to have you back into our lives, Tom.'"

"Would you grow up, Jim? You're not still in high school."

"Well, maybe if you had known him in high school, you'd understand what I'm talking about. This guy is the past master of deceit. He conned his own mother into giving him the bulk of the family trust."

"Which he is trying to pay back, I believe."

"Come on. Wake up! It's all part of the act . . . I just haven't figured out what his next move is. I see him coming back to the family business, and I'm not going to roll over and play dead. I will not—repeat, not—allow him to break my father's heart again."

"Oh please! Don't try to hide your jealousy of your brother behind your father's broken heart. This is not about saving your father from grief. It's about you."

"Okay, okay. I can see how you're so easily taken in by him. You don't know him like I do. You didn't see him sneak out of the house in the middle of the night and then come home drunk or stoned and ask me to cover for him. You didn't see your mother cry herself to sleep at night wondering what became of him. He cheated his way from kindergarten to high school, and when I tried to expose him, I was told to quit being so jealous."

"Maybe you were. . . . All I have ever heard from you is about Tom the louse, Tom the liar, the thief, the drug addict, the alcoholic. Well, you know what? I'm sorry, but you're right: I don't know that guy. The only Tom I see is a man who is trying very hard to put his life back together. The least you can do is not kick him when he's down."

"What do you want me to do? You want me to baby him and coddle him like everyone else around here is doing? You want me to tell him how wonderful he is and forget about all the misery that he caused this family? You want me to start throwing parties for him? Well, no one ever threw a party for me . . . and I've been the good guy. I've been the good guy!"

"What does that mean—you've been the good guy? Do you mean because you haven't made the same mistakes as your brother that you're that much better than him?"

"Come on! You've got to admit that there's a big difference between the things he's done wrong and the things I might have done."

"The difference I see is that one of you is trying to repent and one of you isn't."

"Wait! Since when have I become the big sinner?"

"The minute that you let your pride convince you you're better than somebody else. Sweetheart, just like cocaine and alcohol almost destroyed your brother, jealousy and bitterness are trying to destroy you. Jim, I love you. But you've got to realize that it's not just your brother with the big sins that needs Jesus Christ. You need him just as desperately as any of the rest of us do. If you think that you can overcome this bitterness by yourself, you're just fooling yourself. Tom couldn't overcome his problems alone, and you can't, and I can't. Nobody can. The bottom line is that none of us can make it happily through this life or into the next without the Savior . . . I love you."

29–30. . . . and yet thou never gavest me a kid, that I might make merry with my friends: but as soon as this thy son was come, which hath devoured thy living with harlots, thou hast killed for him the fatted calf.

We see in verse 29 the elder son's scorn in bitingly accusing the father of unfairness. The elder brother says, essentially, "You've never even given me a goat." In Judea, cattle were somewhat scarce, but goats were fairly common. It would take months to fatten a calf, but to find a goat suitable for eating would not require anything out of the ordinary. One scholar has estimated that while the ratio of sheep and goats to cattle was between 2:1 and 7:1, the value of a cow to a goat was 10:1.[38] It is perhaps revealing to note that the elder son has wanted a goat to eat with his friends, not with his family.

The elder brother adds here a detail regarding his

brother's waywardness by suggesting that the prodigal had "devoured thy living with harlots" (v. 30). In truth, we do not know from the scriptural text that the younger son had been immoral in that way. Interestingly, these same charges were made against Jesus, for the Master ate and drank with sinners (Luke 7:34, 39; 15:1–2).

31. And he said unto him, Son, thou art ever with me, and all that I have is thine.

The word the father uses to his elder son means, literally, "child," indicating the father's deep tenderness, affection, and appreciation for the nobility of the elder son's deeds. The inheritance of the elder son, his two-thirds, is still intact and will be his as soon as the father dies. Nothing has been lost.

The Savior's parable of the laborers in the vineyard teaches a similar lesson. Some of the laborers who have worked all day long receive the agreed-upon wage; others who began later in the day (some in the "eleventh hour") receive the same. The former group murmured to the employer about the seeming unfairness of the whole thing. "But he answered one of them, and said, Friend, I do thee no wrong: didst not thou agree with me for a penny? Take that thine is, and go thy way: I will give unto this last, even as unto thee. Is it not lawful for me to do what I will with mine own? Is thine eye evil, because I am good?" (Matthew 20:13–15).

Elder Dallin H. Oaks pointed out that "the Master's reward in the Final Judgment will not be based on how long we have labored in the vineyard. We do not obtain our heavenly reward by punching a time clock. What is essential is that our labors in the workplace of the Lord have caused us to *become* something. For some of us, this requires a longer time than for others. What is important in the end is what we have become by our labors. Many who come in the eleventh hour have been refined and prepared by the Lord in ways other than formal employment in the vineyard. These workers are like the prepared dry mix to which it is only necessary to 'add water'—the perfecting ordinance of baptism and the gift of the Holy Ghost. With that addition—even in the eleventh hour—these workers are in the same state of development and qualified to receive the same reward as those who have labored long in the vineyard.

"This parable teaches us," Elder Oaks continues, "that we should never give up hope and loving associations with family members and friends whose fine qualities (see Moro. 7:5–14) evidence their progress toward what a loving Father would have them become. Similarly, the power of the Atonement and the principle of repentance show that we should never give up on loved ones who now seem to be making many wrong choices."[39]

For the Eternal Father to say to one of us "All that I have is thine" in no way precludes any of the rest of us from inheriting and receiving the same reward of eternal life. There is no ceiling on the number of saved beings. If, in fact, the elder son was true and faithful, we rejoice with him and his parents. We in no way diminish his glory or his eternal attainment by allowing another who was less faithful for a time to repent and come back.

Whether one strays out of ignorance (like the lost sheep), out of neglect (like the lost coin), or knowingly (like the prodigal son), the Almighty, who is a concerned Parent as well as our God, stands ready and willing to receive us back and reinstate us in the royal family.

32. It was meet that we should make merry, and be glad: for this thy brother was dead, and is alive again; and was lost, and is found.

Celebrating the prodigal's return was not just nice and sweet and kind. The father here is saying that it is a divine necessity, the right thing to do on this occasion. It is what he had to do. It is what God would have done. We must reach the point in our spiritual progression where we feel a great longing for the well-being of all our Heavenly Father's children. We must pray for the return of those who have strayed, whether or not they are a part of our immediate or extended family. We must be open and forgiving and responsive to those who seek to make the difficult return home. And we must reach the point where we rejoice with the Father over their return, even, perhaps especially, when their prodigality has affected us directly.

PART THREE

And the son said unto him, Father, I have sinned against heaven,

and in thy sight, and am no more worthy to be called thy son.

But the father said to his servants,

Bring forth the best robe,

and put it on him;

and put a ring on

his hand, and

shoes on his feet:

and bring hither

the fatted calf,

and kill it; and

let us eat, and be

merry: For this my

son was dead, and

is alive again; he was

lost, and is found.

And they began to be merry.

LESSONS FOR LIFE

There is much to be learned from the parable of the prodigal son, so many lessons for life. In that spirit, let us follow Nephi's lead and "liken the scriptures" unto ourselves, "that it might be for our profit and learning" (1 Nephi 19:23).

~

How many of us are startled in our present circumstances by tragedy or trauma, perhaps through the death of a loved one or a crippling injury? How many of us have been awakened by the realization of our plight, combined with a memory of who we were, who we could be, what we might have achieved?

My mind drifts back a few decades to the time just after I

graduated from high school. I had been a pretty good student in high school and had done just about enough work to stay in the A- to B+ grade range. I did study here and there, usually at a time of pressing need; mine was truly a "management by crisis" mode of operation. And then came college. I was a part of the generation of "baby boomers," and many colleges and universities were simply not prepared to receive the huge numbers of entering students. Some institutions therefore determined to weed out systematically those who were not serious students through designated "flunk-out" courses.

Although I was never the brightest kid in school, I did have the capacity to get by—when I chose to apply myself. College life was a brand-new experience. I was all alone. There was no one there to get me out of bed, no one to push me off to school or ask me if I had gone to class and done my homework. I was not prepared for the flexibility and lack of structure and consequently didn't always make it to class.

It doesn't take a nuclear physicist to figure out that class attendance and regular homework are somewhat related to test scores and grades. Let me simply state, to my shame, that I eventually received a letter from the university announcing that because my grades had slipped below the minimum acceptable, I would not be welcome to register for classes the following semester. I was devastated. Shocked. Breathless.

There were many reasons to be upset about flunking out of college, not the least of which was that I would now be available for the draft into the military and thus bound for Vietnam. But something else troubled me—ate away at me—far more than my fear of being drafted. More than anything else, I had let myself down.

I well remember explaining to my parents what had happened, observing the sadness in their eyes, and feeling an almost overwhelming sense of personal disappointment. I knew I would live through the embarrassment of being dropped from college and even survive the regular and insistent questions from those who wondered why I wasn't in school. That would pass. But I sincerely wondered if I would ever regain respect for myself. I knew I had the capacity to do better. I planned to do something with my life, something that would require a good deal of education. Now things were on hold. There were weeks of heartache, and many tears of sorrow were shed. It was a very difficult but very important time for me. I was on the verge of coming to myself after my season of wandering.

Allowing persons dear to us to exercise moral agency can be very painful at times. I remember sitting in a high priests group meeting one Sunday morning. The instructor was delivering a lesson on the plan of salvation and focusing, for the moment, on agency. He had, appropriately, pointed out that there is no mention in scripture of *free* agency, only *moral* agency (D&C 101:78). He then bore his testimony of the centrality of agency, of how awful things would be if we were coerced to do good, and of how grateful we should be for this divinely bestowed gift.

The instructor asked for others in the group to share their own testimonies and feelings of gratitude, which they did for about fifteen minutes. The mood was interrupted quite dramatically when one of the members of the group said, essentially, "Well, that's okay for you folks, and it's fine for me. I'm grateful that I have the right to choose. But to be honest, as far as my family is concerned, sometimes I wish there were no agency. Agency is painful, maybe the most painful thing I can think of. Brethren, I assure you that nothing hurts more than watching your children self-destruct through poor choices."

We were sobered by his comments. I reflected on what this man and his wife had been through over the years. Here was a noble soul, married to a delightful woman after his own good heart. They were not perfect as parents, but it could never be said that they hadn't done their best. They were always at church, held regular family home evenings, and participated in family scripture study and family prayer. Both parents supported the children at school events, athletic events, and cultural events. Several of the children had turned out fine, but a couple of them had serious struggles—drug abuse, dishonesty, and bouts with the law.

I had watched over the years as the buffetings of life and the challenges of child rearing had etched their scars into the countenances of these two godly people. I had watched them try to stay positive, try to face what seemed at the time like insurmountable hurdles, and I knew something of what they felt. There was no bitterness, no lashing out, no desire to curse God, no tendency to give up and throw in the towel, only resignation to life's opposition and a willingness to keep going, with God's help, in spite of their anguish at the poor choices their children made in the name of "freedom."

It is only by coming to him who is the Truth that we gain true freedom (John 8:31–32; 14:6). What many believe to be freedom is actually a form of license that eventually leads to slavery. Elder Boyd K. Packer stated: "Some say that obedience nullifies agency. I would like to point out that obedience is a righteous principle. . . .

"Obedience to God can be the very highest expression of independence. Just think of giving to Him the one thing, the one gift, that He would never take. Think of giving Him that one thing that He would never wrest from you. . . .

"Obedience—that which God will never take by force— He will accept when freely given. And He will then return to you freedom that you can hardly dream of—the freedom to feel and to know, the freedom to do, and the freedom to *be*, at least a thousandfold more than we offer Him. Strangely enough, the key to freedom is obedience."[1]

~

In the words of the immortal Yogi Berra, "It's never over till it's over." While I was serving as a bishop many years ago, a mother and her two children joined the Church. They were enthusiastic beyond description about their newfound faith and dived in with both feet. Or at least they dived in as deeply as they could. The husband and father of the family was not baptized and was not excited about his family's decision. After being in the Church for several months, the mother asked to visit with me. She said: "I think it's time for me to get a divorce. My husband, Fred, not only refuses to get serious about Mormonism, but he has now limited my church attendance. He told me yesterday I could choose which one of the three meetings on Sunday I wanted to attend, but I was only allowed one hour per week of religion."

Now his elder son was in the field: and as he came and drew nigh

to the house, he heard musick and dancing. And he called one of

the servants, and asked what these things meant. And he said

unto him, Thy brother is come; and thy father hath killed the

fatted calf, because he hath received him safe and sound.

I didn't know her husband very well, but it seemed that divorce was not the answer. I suggested that for the time being she work to hold the family together, that she fast and pray regularly for his heart to be softened, and that she do everything in her power to "make home like church"—to be as Christlike and positive and loving as she could be, genuinely so, and demonstrate how the gospel of Jesus Christ had made a difference in her life.

In the months that followed our conversation, little progress seemed to be made. In fact, I remember standing at the pulpit in the chapel on the day their eight-year-old was baptized. I was speaking on the importance of entering the Lord's church and kingdom through baptism and of the vital place of the Holy Spirit in our lives. I turned in the direction of the father of the family as I was bearing my testimony, only to receive the most bitter, angry, and hateful stare I had ever received. The father actually got up before I finished my testimony and stormed out of the room. I thought, "If ever there was a rebellious soul in all the world, we have one here. This clown doesn't have enough decency to sit through a thirty-minute meeting to make his little boy happy. If ever a woman was entitled to a divorce and some peace of mind, this woman is." I am not exactly proud of my feelings on that occasion.

To be honest, if anyone had suggested to me that this pitiful excuse for a man would ever amount to anything, I would have laughed. It is perhaps an indication of my lack of judgment, Christianity, and general perception that the right missionaries eventually came to town, touched this man, baptized him, and set him on course. It was especially sweet to watch him prepare for and receive the ordinances of the temple, return frequently with his sweetheart to the house of the Lord, and become a new creature in Christ. Sarcasm was replaced by sweetness. Macho man was replaced by a priest-hood man, a man of covenant. Whereas before he had ruled his family with an iron hand, he now led lovingly with the rod of iron, the word of God. He is now a gentle and kindly soul who reflects the ways and works of the Master—and a dear and valued friend. Circumstances change. People change.

We just cannot afford to give up on people. It is often the case, when we seem to be at our lowest point, that we are most ready to be turned around in our walk. A colleague shared with me a touching scene in his own family. One of his youngest children, a boy who had begun to wander from the strait path in his teenage years, saw the pain and frustration etched on his father's face one evening. Knowing well that he was the cause of much of his parents' pain, he said,

"Dad, please don't be too upset with me. The Lord's not finished with me yet."

It is so easy for parents of wandering children to take
more than their share of responsibility for the children's waywardness and in some cases to languish in guilt. "As caring
parents," Elder James E. Faust observed, "we do the best we
can. I am hopeful that in parenting God will judge at least
partially by the intent of the parental hearts. . . . Parents have
the obligation to teach, not force, and having prayerfully and
conscientiously taught, parents cannot be answerable for all
their children's conduct. Obedient children do bring honor
to their parents, but it is unfair to judge faithful parents by
the actions of children who will not listen and follow. Parents
do have the obligation to instruct, but children themselves
have a responsibility to listen, to be obedient, and to perform
as they have been taught. . . . To concerned parents I would
paraphrase Winston Churchill: 'Never give up, never give up,
never, never, never.'"[2]

"God has fulfilled His promises to us," President Lorenzo
Snow explained, "and our prospects are grand and glorious.
Yes, in the next life we will have our wives, and our sons and
daughters. If we do not get them all at once, we will have
them some time, for every knee shall bow and every tongue
shall confess that Jesus is the Christ. You that are mourning

about your children straying away will have your sons and your daughters. If you succeed in passing through these trials and afflictions and receive a resurrection, you will, by the power of the Priesthood, work and labor, as the Son of God has, until you get all your sons and daughters in the path of exaltation and glory. This is just as sure as that the sun rose this morning over yonder mountains. Therefore, mourn not because all your sons and daughters do not follow in the path that you have marked out to them, or give heed to your counsels. Inasmuch as we succeed in securing eternal glory, and stand as saviors, and as kings and priests to our God, we will save our posterity. . . .

"God will have His own way in His own time, and He will accomplish His purposes in the salvation of His sons and daughters. . . .

"God bless you, brethren and sisters. *Do not be discouraged* is the word I wish to pass to you; but remember that righteousness and joy in the Holy Ghost is what you and I have the privilege of possessing at all times."[3]

And so, because we are mortal, because we are human, because we cannot see the end from the beginning, when a child wanders we fret and ache and sometimes despair. But there is hope. There is reason to hold on, to hope on.

President Gordon B. Hinckley, in addressing the Saints in

Great Britain, said: "May you be blessed, each of you. May there be love and peace and gladness in your homes. I leave my blessing upon you. May there be food on your table, clothing on your backs, shelter over your heads and a sense of security and peace and love among your children, precious children every one of them, even those who may have strayed. I hope you don't lose patience with them; I hope you go on praying for them, and I don't hesitate to promise that if you do so, the Lord will touch their hearts and bring them back to you with love and respect and appreciation."[4]

As Elder Dallin H. Oaks explained, although we have been asked by the Lord and his servants to make intermediate judgments every day of our lives—including what is good and what is evil, as well as what we should and should not do—we must not place ourselves in the inappropriate position of judging another in that we assume that we know his or her final outcome in the Father's plan, particularly whether he or she will be saved or damned hereafter. Elder Oaks pointed out that "we presume to make final judgments whenever we proclaim that any particular person is going to hell (or to heaven) for a particular act or as of a particular time. When we do this—and there is great temptation to do so—we hurt ourselves and the person we pretend to judge."

Elder Oaks added that "we must refrain from making

final judgments on people because we lack the knowledge and the wisdom to do so. We would even apply the wrong standards. The world's way is to judge competitively between winners and losers. The Lord's way of final judgment will be to apply His perfect knowledge of the law a person has received and to judge on the basis of that person's circumstances, motives, and actions throughout his or her entire life."[5] "There is never a time," Joseph Smith declared, "when the spirit is too old to approach God. All are within the reach of pardoning mercy, who have not committed the unpardonable sin."[6]

In that spirit, we need to be careful about condemning outright—or, at best, being overly suspicious about—those circumstances in which desperation impels a wandering sheep to search out God. The consensus among onlookers might be that these kinds of conversions don't last, but do we really know for sure? Dare we judge? We cannot afford to treat lightly any repentance, any effort to return. While remorse—in the case of the parable of the prodigal son, finding oneself in a degraded condition—may not of itself constitute full and complete repentance, it is often a significant part, a real beginning.

In addition, in some cases we must allow God, who like the father in the parable runs out to welcome the prodigal, to find us. For example, where was the repentance of the lost sheep or the lost coin? In both of those parables, the lost items were simply *found*. The work of salvation in behalf of my soul is a team effort between God and me.

In seeking to console the parents of rebellious sons and daughters, Elder Orson F. Whitney said: "You parents of the wilful and the wayward! Don't give them up. Don't cast them off. *They are not utterly lost. The Shepherd will find his sheep.* They were his before they were yours—long before he entrusted them to your care; and you cannot begin to love them as he loves them. *They have but strayed in ignorance from the Path of Right, and God is merciful to ignorance. Only the fulness of knowledge brings the fulness of accountability.* Our Heavenly Father is far more merciful, infinitely more charitable, than even the best of his servants, and the Everlasting Gospel is mightier in power to save than our narrow finite minds can comprehend."[7]

Further, we must be the kind of people with whom a wanderer would feel comfortable should he or she choose to return. If one who has descended to the depths should find it within him or her to come back to the path, those who are waiting must also be welcoming. Philip Yancey has noted that "the more unsavory the characters, the more at ease they seemed to feel around Jesus. People like these found Jesus appealing: a Samaritan social outcast, a military officer of the tyrant Herod, a quisling tax collector, a recent hostess to seven demons.

"In contrast, Jesus got a chilly response from more respectable types. Pious Pharisees thought him uncouth and worldly, a rich young ruler walked away shaking his head, and even the open-minded Nicodemus sought a meeting under the cover of darkness. . . .

"Somehow we have created a community of respectability in the church," Yancey warned. "The down-and-out, who flocked to Jesus when he lived on earth, no longer feel welcome. How did Jesus, the only perfect person in history, manage to attract the notoriously imperfect? And what keeps us from following in his steps today?"[8]

In short, we need to allow people to change, to be better, to improve, no matter what we may remember about them. That requires an open and loving countenance, a non-judgmental manner, an absence of self-righteousness. Elder Jeffrey R. Holland wrote: "I once knew a boy who had no father and precious few of the other blessings of life. The young men in his community found it easy to tease and taunt and bully him. And in the process of it all he made some mistakes, though I cannot believe his mistakes were more serious than those of his Latter-day Saint friends who made life so miserable for him. He began to drink and smoke, and gospel principles that had never meant much to him now meant even less. He had been cast in a role by Latter-day Saint friends who should have known better, and he began to play the part perfectly. Soon he drank even more, went to school even less, and went to church not at all. Then one day he was gone. Some said they thought he had joined the army.

"That was about 1959 or so. Fifteen or sixteen years later he came home. At least he tried to come home. He had found the significance of the gospel in his life. He had married a wonderful girl, and they had a beautiful family. But he discovered something upon his return. He had changed, but some of his old friends hadn't—and they were unwilling to let him escape his past.

"This was hard for him and hard for his family. They bought a little home and started a small business, but they struggled both personally and professionally and finally moved away. For reasons that don't need to be detailed here, the story goes on to a very unhappy ending. He died not long after, at age forty-four. That's too young to die these days, and it's certainly too young to die away from home.

"When a battered, weary swimmer tries valiantly to get back to shore after having fought strong winds and rough waves that he should never have challenged in the first place, those of us who might have had better judgment (or perhaps just better luck) ought not to row out to his side, beat him with our oars, and shove his head back underwater. That's not what boats were made for."⁹

"All who are active," Elder Vaughn J. Featherstone pointed out, "have someone close who may be inactive, indifferent, or clothed in transgression's soiled robes. They need the sweet, abiding love of a compassionate parent or loving brother or sister. Jesus will bless every member of the Church who will go out and bring someone back."¹⁰

～

There are some hungers that cannot be filled, some sorrows that cannot be handled, without God. "For my people have committed two evils," Jehovah said in regard to ancient Israel, "they have forsaken me the fountain of living waters, and hewed them out cisterns, broken cisterns, that can hold no water" (Jeremiah 2:13). All people thirst, even if they don't realize it. Most people pursue their quest for the living water inappropriately—they choose alternate paths, often irresponsible and usually unproductive and empty strategies. The world may have its agenda; the Savior has another approach entirely. There is safety and security only in discovering and implementing the Lord's way.

C. S. Lewis taught that people everywhere seek to "invent some sort of happiness for themselves outside God, apart from God. And out of that hopeless attempt has come nearly all that we call human history—money, poverty, ambition, war, prostitution, classes, empires, slavery—the long terrible story of man trying to find something other than God which will make him happy.

"The reason why it can never succeed is this. God made us: invented us as a man invents an engine. A car is made to run on gasoline, and it would not run properly on anything else. Now God designed the human machine to run on Himself. He Himself is the fuel our spirits were designed to burn, or the food our spirits were designed to feed on. There is no other. That is why it is just no good asking God to make us happy in our own way without bothering about religion. God cannot give us a happiness and peace apart from Himself, because it is not there. There is no such thing."[11]

~

Unlike other parables Jesus told, the parable of the prodigal son is not a story about a bad guy and a good guy. *Only the father is good* (Matthew 19:17). "For the father, the sons

And he was angry, and would not go in: therefore came his father out, and intreated him. And he answering said to his father, Lo, these many years do I serve thee, neither transgressed I at any time thy commandment: and yet thou never gavest me a kid, that I might make merry with my friends: but as soon as this thy son was come, which hath devoured thy living with harlots, thou hast killed for him the fatted calf. And he said unto him, Son, thou art ever with me, and all that I have is thine.

cannot be placed on a moral scale and then the returning prodigal, on account of his confession, pronounced better and accepted but the older brother pronounced worse and rejected. The non-prodigal is *good* in that he has remained, worked, obeyed, but he is *bad* in that he was too concerned with the 'rules' and has not received his brother back and rejoiced. The prodigal is *bad* in that he has gone and *good* in that he has returned and confessed. Both are loved, however, irrespective of their goodness or badness."[12]

Elder Marvin J. Ashton commented on the love of the father in these words: "Please weigh the impact of the father's response once more. He saw the son coming; he ran to him; he kissed him; he placed his best robe on him; he killed the fatted calf; and they made merry together. This self-declared 'nobody' was his son; he was 'dead, and is alive again; he was lost, and is found.'

"In the father's joy he also taught well his older, bewildered son that he too was someone. 'Son, thou art ever with me, and all that I have is thine.' Contemplate, if you will, the depth—yes, even the eternal proportions—of 'all that I have is thine.' I declare with all the strength I possess that we have a Heavenly Father who claims and loves all of us regardless of where our steps have taken us. You are his son and you are his daughter, and he loves you."[13] Even though this story has been called the parable of the prodigal son, it might more appropriately be called the parable of the loving father. It is the father, not the younger son, who is the hero of the story.

Richard Rice has written: "If the first two parables [the lost sheep and the lost coin] show us how much like our feelings God's feelings are, the last one discloses a vast difference between them. The wayward son deserves to be rejected. At the least he merits a public rebuke. But instead of humiliating his son, the father humiliates himself by unceremoniously running to him—in full view of curious villagers, no doubt—embracing him, restoring him instantly to his honored position in the family and then even throwing a party to celebrate his return. There is not a trace of recrimination or a hint of resentment in his actions. To rejoice with the return of an irresponsible, insensitive son, rather than turn him away or shower him with reproach, contradicts normal behavior. It reveals a depth of feeling that transcends our natural human emotions." Truly, "the joy of the father mystifies us. It is as unexpected as it is profound."[14]

〜

God and the angels in heaven rejoice—and they call upon us to do the same—when lost sheep are retrieved into the fold. This supernal message is echoed in all scripture. As pointed out earlier, a central message in the allegory of Zenos (Jacob 5) is that Israel's God simply will not let Israel go. And what is true of a nation is equally true of individuals. Few of us in this life will through our sins place ourselves beyond the pale of saving grace.

God cherishes each one of us, not simply because we are his children (which is itself a powerful incentive for him to save as many as possible), but also because our Lord and Savior has paid an infinite price for us. We are a peculiar, meaning a purchased, people. We have been redeemed not through an exchange of corruptible things but instead "with the precious blood of Christ, as of a lamb without blemish and without spot" (1 Peter 1:18–19). Something so costly cannot be ignored or treated lightly.

"Remember the worth of souls is great in the sight of God; for, behold, the Lord your Redeemer suffered death in the flesh; wherefore he suffered the pain of all men, that all men might repent and come unto him. And he hath risen again from the dead, that he might bring all men unto him, on conditions of repentance. And how great is his joy in the soul that repenteth! Wherefore, you are called to cry repentance unto this people. And if it so be that you should labor all your days in crying repentance unto this people, and bring, save it be one soul unto me, how great shall be your joy with him in the kingdom of my Father! And now, if your joy will be great with one soul that you have brought unto me into the kingdom of my Father, how great will be your joy if you should bring many souls unto me!" (D&C 18:10–16).

In speaking of what drew the prodigal homeward, Elder Marvin J. Ashton asked: "Could there have been moments, as he gleaned the fields for husks to eat, when he longed for the security, safety, and acceptance he'd had before? Might he have been deeply homesick? Repentant, and hoping his father would accept him as a servant, he finally returned home. His father rejoiced, welcoming him back with open arms and complete acceptance. He no doubt knew that welcoming his wayward son was crucial if he hoped to ever return to his heavenly home."[15]

While our tears and our hard work allow us to evidence the depth of our contrition and the seriousness of our commitment, it is not our good work alone that wins the favor of the Father; it is the work of our Divine Redeemer. Aaron, son of King Mosiah, taught that "since man had fallen he could not merit anything of himself; but the sufferings and death of Christ atone for their sins, through faith and repentance" (Alma 22:14). Lehi proclaimed that "there is no flesh that can dwell in the presence of God, save it be through the merits, and mercy, and grace of the Holy Messiah" (2 Nephi

2:8). Indeed, it is only by relying wholly—relying alone—upon the merits and grace of the Savior that we can ever hope to qualify to go where God is (2 Nephi 31:19; Moroni 6:4). As Lehi taught Jacob, "I know that thou art redeemed, because of the righteousness of thy Redeemer" (2 Nephi 2:3). Our Advocate with the Father pleads our cause on the basis of *his* suffering and death and mighty merits before God (D&C 45:3–5).

~

There are limits, not necessarily to God's mercy but to the extent to which mercy can temper justice. Thus we must never convey the idea that individuals may sin freely in order that grace may abound (Romans 6:1–2). In speaking of very serious sins, President Joseph F. Smith explained that a person can and will be forgiven if he repents: "The blood of Christ will make him free, and will wash him clean, though his sins be as scarlet; but all this will not return to him any loss sustained, nor place him on an equal footing with his neighbor who has kept the commandents of the better law. Nor will it place him in the position where he would have been, had he not committed wrong."[16] This is why we teach that prevention is far, far better than redemption. Stated differently, it is always better to prepare and prevent than to repair and repent. Though we rejoice in the cleansing powers of the blood of our Redeemer, we must, as President Harold B. Lee counseled, impress the members of the Church "with the awfulness of sin rather than to content ourselves with merely teaching the way of repentance."[17]

I have a feeling if we were to interview the prodigal son and ask him a few thoughtful questions about his period of straying as well as his return, he would be the first to admit that sinning is not the way to go. He would no doubt speak of the painful loss of the Spirit of God, the painful loss of association with family and friends, and the painful realization that while he was sinning he was not learning and growing and developing. "As far as we degenerate from God," Joseph Smith declared, "we descend to the devil and lose knowledge, and without knowledge we cannot be saved, and while our hearts are filled with evil, and we are studying evil, there is no room in our hearts for good, or studying good."[18]

~

In order for our Heavenly Father to receive us back, his Beloved Son had to die a shameful death. The cost of our being restored to the royal family is borne not by us but by the Father and the Son. Alma testified that the Great Jehovah would come to earth, take upon himself our pains, afflictions, temptations, sicknesses, infirmities, and even death, "that his bowels may be filled with mercy, according to the flesh, that he may know according to the flesh how to succor his people according to their infirmities" (Alma 7:11–12). Jesus Christ, our Advocate, knows "the weakness of man and how to succor them who are tempted" (D&C 62:1). To succor is to help, to assist, to tenderly care for. More specifically, it is "to run to, or run to support; hence, to help or relieve when in difficulty, want or distress; to assist and deliver from suffering."[19] Like the father in the parable, Jesus and the Father run to meet us—that is, they succor us—as we evidence our sincere desire to return home.

As the scapegoat, the Master bears the shame of it all for us. He makes to us an offer that only the foolish and extremely nearsighted would not accept: He proposes what has been called the great exchange. Jesus offers, to those who enter into the gospel covenant, to take upon himself the effects of our sins and to transfer to us his righteousness. "For he [God the Father] hath made him [Christ the Son] to be sin for us, who knew no sin; that we might be made the righteousness of God in him" (2 Corinthians 5:21). He who was appointed to "taste death for every man" (Hebrews 2:9) "hath redeemed us from the curse of the law, being made a curse for us" (Galatians 3:13).

~

Each of us, at one time or another, plays three roles in life: the younger son, the older son, and the father. In speaking of the parable of the prodigal son, Elder Gordon B. Hinckley said: "I ask you to read that story. Every parent ought to read it again and again. It is large enough to encompass every household, and enough larger than that to encompass all mankind, for are we not all prodigal sons and daughters who need to repent and partake of the forgiving mercy of our Heavenly Father and then follow his example?"[20]

Sadly, there are times—far too many of them—when we are dutiful, faithful, dependable, and consistent in our contributions but lack that quality of mercy and kindness and compassion that would allow us to reflect and extend the hand of forgiveness and fellowship to those who wander.

Elder Neal A. Maxwell spoke of what Martha, sister of Mary and Lazarus, must have felt (Luke 10:38–42), as well as what the elder brother of the prodigal son seems to have felt. Elder Maxwell observed: "How many of us have privately identified, at least at first blush, not only with Martha but also with the stay-at-home brother of the prodigal son? If so, some introspection may be useful. Do we feel put upon at times, as Martha must have done, in busy situations in which nobody appears to appreciate what we are doing and others seem heedless of the many tasks that must be done? *Do we feel the prodigals get attention that really should be ours, and also that they seem to have their cake and eat it, too?* There are even deeper implications, but the thrust of these implications may be our inability to love. For true love can help us to see what is most needed and what is most important. And true love can gladly and spontaneously respond when others come to their senses. Those of us who 'are in the field,' who hear the sounds of rejoicing, can stay outside and withhold our warmth. But if it is our Father's quiet respect we really want (since we have his love) and not the attention-getting of receiving 'a fatted calf,' we will do better not to require our Father or his servants to come out and entreat us. For while our loyalty to Him is not at issue, our degree of maturity is. It is as if, child-like, we demand 'equal time' and attention, and our Father says, 'If it is reassurance you need, you shall have it; but would that you were more ready for the full burdens of leadership.'"[21]

Elder Boyd K. Packer told a story that demonstrates this need in our lives to glory in the return of those who stray. He was serving as a mission president at the time. "I needed a new assistant and had prayed much about the matter. I then called zone conferences, where I met and interviewed every missionary, always with the thought in my mind, 'Is this the man?' The answer finally came: 'This is the man.' He was appointed. He had been permitted to come on a mission only after some considerable shaping up to become eligible.

"After the announcement one of the zone leaders came to see me privately. He came from the same community in the West as did the new assistant. He was obviously disturbed. His first question was, 'Do you really know the elder you have appointed as your assistant?'

"'Yes, Elder. I know all that you know about him, and a good deal more,' was my answer.

"'Why, then, was *he* appointed your assistant?'

"I pondered for a moment and then said, 'Elder, why don't you ask the question that you came to ask?'

"'What do you mean?'

"'Ask the question that is really on your mind,' I encouraged.

"'But I did,' he said.

"'No,' I said. 'There is another question. The thing that is on your mind is not 'Why did you appoint him as your assistant'; it is 'Why did you not appoint me?'

"Now please understand. I thought his unexpressed question to be a very logical and sensible one. For it included this thought: 'Here I am. I have worked as hard as I know

how to work. All my life I have been a straight arrow. I have
not rebelled nor been disobedient. I have prepared myself for
a mission in every way I know how to prepare. I have been
trained, and I have studied. I have respected my parents and
my bishop, and I have presided over my quorums. And here
I am a missionary.

"'Now another, whose path has been crooked, who has
skipped meetings and dabbled in mischief, who winked at
restriction and snickered at obedience, has been elevated
above me.' I had sympathy for this young man and admired
him greatly for his courage to speak.

"'If you should ask why you were not chosen,' I said, 'I
would have to answer, "I do not know, Elder." I only know
that he was chosen. Perhaps he may fail. But at least I know
he is the one with the combination of talents and ability and
qualities best calculated to get done what the office needs at
the moment.

"'This is no reflection upon you. You may yet preside
over him and many above him. You may be his bishop or his
stake president. You may preside over the Church. I do not
know. But his call is no reflection upon you. Do not be injured
by it.'

"'Go back to work and serve the Lord. Sustain him,' I
counseled. 'Your contest is not with him but with yourself.'

"And then I gently added, 'You may have a bit of repenting to do.'

"Some weeks later I saw him again. This time he said with simple assurance, 'I know one reason why he was appointed your assistant. So that I could learn the greatest lesson that I have ever learned in my life.'"[22]

We must first learn what being a true son or daughter means before we can aspire one day to being like the waiting and welcoming father. Leon Morris wrote that "the elder son was conscious of his own rectitude. He was completely self-righteous. He saw himself as the model son, but [his use of the language] 'to serve as a slave' . . . gives him away. He did not really understand what being a son means. That is perhaps why he did not understand what being a father means."[23]

In that light, Henri Nouwen pointed out: "A child does not remain a child. A child becomes an adult. An adult becomes father and mother. When the prodigal son returns home, he returns not to remain a child, but to claim his sonship and become a father himself. As the returned child of God who is invited to resume my place in my Father's home, the challenge now, yes the call, is to become the Father myself." That is, "there is a call beyond the call to return. It is the call to become the Father who welcomes home and calls for a celebration. Having reclaimed my sonship, I now have to claim fatherhood. . . .

"My final vocation is indeed to become like the Father and to live out his divine compassion in my daily life. Though I am both the younger son and the elder son, I am not to remain them, but to become the Father. No father or mother ever became father or mother without having been son or daughter, but every son and daughter has to consciously choose to step beyond their childhood and become father and mother for others." Finally, "becoming like the heavenly Father is not just one important aspect of Jesus' teaching, it is the very heart of his message. . . .

" . . . Spiritual fatherhood has nothing to do with power or control. It is a fatherhood of compassion. And I have to keep looking at the father embracing the prodigal son to catch a glimpse of this."[24]

∾

Is the message of this parable really fair to all those who have been faithful all along? Let me ask this another way: Would I have attended the banquet for the returning prodigal? Would I honor someone who had so blatantly dishonored his father? Would I perhaps worry that I would be encouraging waywardness and irresponsibility? Would the party seem to cancel out the seriousness of all the old sins? I repeat what Joseph Smith taught: "God does not look on sin with allowance, but when men have sinned, there must be allowance made for them."[25] Stated bluntly, all of us are guilty of sin. All of us are in need of pardoning mercy. All of us fall short of the divine standard.

During a long day of debate with his opponents, Jesus delivered the following parable: "A certain man had two sons; and he came to the first, and said, Son, go work to day in my vineyard. He [the son] answered and said, I will not: but afterward he repented, and went. And he came to the second, and said likewise. And he [the second son] answered and said, I go sir: and went not. Whether of them twain did the will of his father?" (Matthew 21:28–31). We "may wonder why this story does not include a third son who said, 'I will' and kept his word. Perhaps it is because this story characterizes humanity, and we all fall short (Rom. 3:23). Thus Jesus could describe only two kinds of religious people: those who pretend to be obedient but are actually rebels, and those who begin as rebels but repent."[26]

Inasmuch as each of us is a recipient of unending and unmerited grace, how can we, in the spirit of Christian charity—or in the attitude of sane discourse—speak of the Lord's pardoning mercy toward prodigal sons and daughters as unfair? Of course it's unfair. It's all unfair! That a pure and innocent man should suffer and agonize over others' transgressions is not fair. That he who had never taken a backward step should tread the winepress alone, "even the winepress of the fierceness of the wrath of Almighty God" (D&C 76:107; 88:106) and thereby descend below all things (D&C 88:6), is not fair. That the lowly Nazarene should be subjected to the ignominy and unspeakable torture of crucifixion is unfair.

But the plan of the Father is not a plan of fairness, at least as we judge fairness from our limited perspective; it is a plan of mercy. The Father and the Son love us in ways that we cannot comprehend. They will do all that is within the bounds of propriety to save as many of the sons and daughters of Adam and Eve as will be saved. "God's mercy, indeed, is as foolish as a shepherd who abandons 99 sheep to save one, as a woman who turns her house upside down to recover a paltry sum, and as a Jewish father who joyfully welcomes home his wastrel son who has become a Gentile."[27]

President J. Reuben Clark Jr. spoke of the goodness of our God: "I feel that [the Lord] will give that punishment which is the very least that our transgression will justify. . . .

" . . . I believe that when it comes to making the rewards for our good conduct, he will give us the maximum that it is possible to give."[28]

PART FOUR

It was meet that we should make merry, and be glad:

for this thy brother was dead, and is alive again;

and was lost, and is found.

CONCLUSION

mong Nephi's closing words to us are these tender thoughts: "I glory in plainness; I glory in truth; I glory in my Jesus, for he hath redeemed my soul from hell. I have charity for my people, and great faith in Christ that I shall meet many souls spotless at his judgment-seat." Further, "I pray the Father in the name of Christ that many of us, if not all, may be saved in his kingdom at that great and last day" (2 Nephi 33:6–7, 12). Likewise, Mormon mused: "And may God grant, in his great fulness, that men might be brought unto repentance and good works, that they might be restored unto grace for grace, according to their works. And I would that all men might be saved" (Helaman 12:24–25).

Surely any person who has experienced firsthand the love

of God, who has confessed and repented and enjoyed thereafter the marvelous miracle of forgiveness—and this includes
all of us—can identify with the pain and distress and feeling
of lostness known to the prodigal. Although clearly there are
some sins against the law of God that are more serious than
others and thus require more time and energy of soul to
repent of, in a broader way all of us know something about
what it is like to be imperfect, to make mistakes, to sin, to
wander, even if only for a short time. And if we have experienced the change of heart that evidences the effect of the
atoning blood of Christ on our lives, then hopefully our
desire, like Nephi and Mormon, is that all who have strayed
may return and be renewed, no matter the depth of their dis-
grace.

We know, to be sure, that not everyone will make it. Not
all of our Father's children will inherit eternal life in his
"many mansions" (John 14:2). As Mormon went on to say,
"We read that in the great and last day there are some who
shall be cast out, yea, who shall be cast off from the presence
of the Lord; yea, who shall be consigned to a state of endless
misery, fulfilling the words which say: They that have done
good shall have everlasting life; and they that have done evil
shall have everlasting damnation. And thus it is. Amen"
(Helaman 12:25–26). But that does not preclude any or all of

us from hoping and praying and ministering and welcoming those who come to themselves and choose to return.

Sadly, as Richard John Neuhaus stated, "The hope that all may be saved . . . offends some Christians. It is as though salvation were a zero-sum proposition, as though there is only so much to go around, as though God's grace to others will somehow diminish our portion of grace. . . .

" . . . If we love others, it seems that we must hope that, in the end, they will be saved. We must hope that all will one day hear the words of Christ, 'Today you will be with me in paradise.' Given the evidence of Scripture and tradition, we cannot deny that hell exists. We can, however, hope that hell is empty. We cannot know that, but we can hope it is the case."[1]

Our God is all-powerful, all-knowing, and all-loving. There is no end to his capacity to reach out, to reclaim, to reinstate. After having read the parable of the prodigal son, Elder Gordon B. Hinckley extended this invitation and welcome to those who have left the fold: "To you, my brethren and sisters, who have taken your spiritual inheritance and left, and now find an emptiness in your lives, the way is open for your return.

"Note the words of the parable of the Prodigal Son: 'And when he came to himself.'

"Have you not also reflected on your condition and circumstances, and longed to return?

"The boy in the parable wanted only to be a servant in his father's house, but his father, seeing him afar off, ran to meet him and kissed him, put a robe on his back, a ring on his hand, and shoes on his feet, and had a feast prepared for him.

"So it will be with you. If you will take the first timid step to return, you will find open arms to greet you and warm friends to make you welcome.

"I think I know why some of you left," Elder Hinckley said. "You were offended by a thoughtless individual who injured you, and you mistook his actions as representative of the Church. Or you may have moved from an area where you were known to an area where you were largely alone, and there grew up with only little knowledge of the Church.

"Or you may have been drawn to other company or habits which you felt were incompatible with association in the Church. Or you may have felt yourself wiser in the wisdom of the world than those of your Church associates, and with some air of disdain, withdrawn yourself from their company.

"I am not here to dwell on the reasons. I hope you will not. Put the past behind you. . . .

"Try it. There is everything to gain and nothing to lose. Come back, my friends. There is more of peace to be found in the Church than you have known in a long while. There are many whose friendship you will come to enjoy. There is reading to be done, instruction to be received, discussions in which to participate that will stretch your minds and feed your spirits.

"The quiet longings of your heart will be fulfilled. The emptiness you have known for so long will be replaced with a fulness of joy."[2]

Unlike a fairy tale, the parable of the prodigal son does not end " . . . and they lived happily ever after." How does it end? Did the older brother close his ears to the loving counsel of his father, steel himself against compassion, and live and die an angry and bitter man? Or was he deeply touched by the love of his father—pure love for him, as well as for his returning brother? Did he allow the power of the Almighty to transform his soul, reshape his attitudes and actions, and make him into an instrument of divine love? In fact, this is an open-ended story, one each of us must finish in our own personal lives.

I testify of the reality of the hope and the beauty of the promises that come through the parable of the prodigal son. We cannot give up hope for those who stray. We must not.

President J. Reuben Clark Jr. offered this comforting assurance and challenge: "It is my hope and my belief that the
Lord never permits the light of faith wholly to be extin-
guished in any human heart, however faint the light may
glow. The Lord has provided that there shall still be there a
spark which, with teaching, with the spirit of righteousness,
with love, with tenderness, with example, with living the
Gospel, shall brighten and glow again, however darkened the
mind may have been. And if we shall fail so to reach those
among us of our own whose faith has dwindled low, we shall
fail in one of the main things which the Lord expects at our
hands."[3]

Like the prodigal, each of us is staggered by the infinite
love of God the Father and the patience and tender regard of
his Beloved Son, Jesus Christ. Truly, we stand all amazed at
the love Jesus offers us.

> When I survey the wondrous cross on which
>   the Prince of glory died,
> My richest gain I count but loss, and pour
>   contempt on all my pride.
> Forbid it, Lord, that I should boast, save in the
>   death of Christ, my God!
> All the vain things that charm me most, I sac-
>   rifice them to his blood.
> See, from his head, his hands, his feet, sorrow
>   and love flow mingled down!

Did ever such love and sorrow meet, or thorns
  compose so rich a crown?
Were the whole realm of nature mine, that
  were a present far too small;
Love, so amazing, so divine, demands my
  soul, my life, my all![4]

I bear witness of the goodness of God and of the infinite mercy of him who was sent to earth "to preach good tidings unto the meek; . . . to bind up the brokenhearted, to proclaim liberty to the captives, and the opening of the prison to them that are bound" (Isaiah 61:1). In 1942 C. S. Lewis wrote the following in a letter: "No *amount* of falls will really undo us if we keep on picking ourselves up each time. We shall of course be very muddy and tattered children by the time we reach home. But the bathrooms are all ready, the towels put out, and the clean clothes in the airing cupboard. The only fatal thing is to lose one's temper and give it up."[5]

"Thanks be to God, which giveth us the victory through our Lord Jesus Christ" (1 Corinthians 15:57). As a result of the greatest act of condescension, mercy, and divine love in all eternity—the Infinite Atonement—Jesus the Christ "hath abolished death, and hath brought life and immortality to light through the gospel" (2 Timothy 1:10). He has come, and he will come again.

And when he comes, the King of Love will gather to his side those who love him and trust in his goodness, those who know their limitations and their weakness, those who plead for his tender mercy. He will not only teach the brightest and most intellectually gifted among us, the articulate and the impressive, but he will call forward those who meekly acknowledge their ignorance, those who are open, teachable, and willing to learn from him and from his chosen servants. He will receive those whose walk has been steady and whose witness has been solid and secure. And he will embrace those who have believed on the testimony of chosen vessels, those who cry out, "Lord, I believe; help thou mine unbelief" (Mark 9:24).

The Good Shepherd reaches out to the willful and the wanton, the proud and the judgmental, the lonely and the languishing. His is an everlasting appeal and invitation: "Come unto me, all ye that labour and are heavy laden, and I will give you rest. Take my yoke upon you, and learn of me; for I am meek and lowly in heart: and ye shall find rest unto your souls. For my yoke is easy, and my burden is light" (Matthew 11:28–30).

"Come," he beckons to the returning prodigals, "we are going home to the waiting Father."[6]

NOTES

PART ONE

INTRODUCTION

1. Smith, *Teachings*, 218.

2. Hunter, Conference Report, October 1979, 93.

3. Yancey, *Jesus I Never Knew*, 174–75.

4. Smith, *Teachings*, 240–41.

5. Yancey, *Jesus I Never Knew*, 89.

6. Jeremias, *Parables of Jesus*, 132.

7. Hultgren, *Parables of Jesus*, 470.

8. Smith, *Teachings*, 276–77.

9. Ibid., 277.

10. Ibid., 241.

11. McKay, *Gospel Ideals*, 534–35.

12. Smith, *Teachings*, 277–78.

13. McKay, *Gospel Ideals*, 536–37.

14. "Come, Thou Fount of Every Blessing," *Hymns*, 1948, no. 70.

PART TWO
THE PARABLE AND COMMENTARY

1. McKay, *Gospel Ideals*, 537.

2. Thielicke, *Waiting Father*, 20–21; italics in original.

3. Nouwen, *Return of the Prodigal Son*, 35.

4. Bailey, *Poet and Peasant*, 161–62.

5. Nouwen, *Return of the Prodigal Son*, 36.

6. Volf, *Exclusion and Embrace*, 158; italics in original.

7. "O My Father," *Hymns*, 1985, no. 292.

8. Maxwell, Conference Report, October 2000, 47.

9. Hultgren, *Parables of Jesus*, 75.

10. Ibid., 75.

11. Nouwen, *Return of the Prodigal Son*, 46–47.

12. Volf, *Exclusion and Embrace*, 158–59; italics added.

13. Neuhaus, *Death on a Friday Afternoon*, 4.

14. Maxwell, Conference Report, October 2000, 47.

15. Benson, *Teachings*, 72.

16. Marshall, *Gospel of Luke*, 609–10.

17. Hultgren, *Parables of Jesus*, 78.

18. Ibid., 78.

19. Bailey, *Poet and Peasant*, 181–82.

20. Ibid., 181, n. 177.

21. Ibid., 182.

22. Hultgren, *Parables of Jesus*, 79.

23. McConkie, *Mortal Messiah*, 3:251.

24. Jeremias, *Parables of Jesus*, 130.

25. Marshall, *Gospel of Luke*, 610.

26. Ibid., 610–11.

27. *New Jerome Biblical Commentary*, 707.

28. *Hymns*, 1985, no. 221.

29. Stuy, *Collected Discourses*, 5:52.

30. Bailey, *Poet and Peasant,* 192.

31. Volf, *Exclusion and Embrace,* 161–62.

32. Bailey, *Finding the Lost,* 171.

33. Bailey, *Poet and Peasant,* 194.

34. Hultgren, *Parables of Jesus,* 80.

35. Stuy, *Collected Discourses,* 5:52–53.

36. Barclay, *Parables of Jesus,* 186.

37. Bonneville Communications, 1990.

38. Hultgren, *Parables of Jesus,* 81, n. 48.

39. Oaks, Conference Report, October 2000, 44.

PART THREE

LESSONS FOR LIFE

1. Packer, *"That All May Be Edified,"* 255–56.

2. Faust, Conference Report, October 1984, 73–74.

3. Stuy, *Collected Discourses,* 3:364–65.

4. *Church News,* 2 September 1995, 4.

5. Oaks, "'Judge Not' and Judging," 7–8.

6. Smith, *Teachings,* 191.

7. Whitney, Conference Report, April 1929, 110; italics added.

8. Yancey, *Jesus I Never Knew,* 147–48.

9. Holland, *However Long and Hard the Road,* 70–71.

10. Featherstone, Conference Report, October 1982, 105.

11. Lewis, *Mere Christianity,* 54.

12. Volf, *Exclusion and Embrace,* 165, n. 44; italics in original.

13. Ashton, Conference Report, April 1973, 24.

14. Rice, "Biblical Support for a New Perspective," 41–42.

15. Ashton, Conference Report, October 1992, 29.

16. Smith, *Gospel Doctrine,* 374; see also Kimball, *Miracle of Forgiveness,* 310–11.

17. Lee, *Decisions for Successful Living*, 88.

18. Smith, *Teachings*, 217.

19. *Webster's American Dictionary of the English Language*, s.v. "succor."

20. Hinckley, Conference Report, October 1980, 88.

21. Maxwell, *"For the Power Is in Them,"* 11–12; italics added.

22. Packer, *"That All May Be Edified,"* 51–52; italics in original.

23. Morris, *Gospel According to St. Luke*, 267.

24. Nouwen, *Return of the Prodigal Son*, 118–19, 121, 125, 127.

25. Smith, *Teachings*, 240–41.

26. MacArthur, *Gospel According to Jesus*, 183–84.

27. *New Jerome Biblical Commentary*, 707.

28. Clark, "As Ye Sow," 7.

PART FOUR

CONCLUSION

1. Neuhaus, *Death on a Friday Afternoon*, 57, 61.

2. Hinckley, Conference Report, October 1976, 142–44.

3. Clark, Conference Report, October 1936, 114.

4. "When I Survey the Wondrous Cross," *Praise!* no. 224.

5. Lewis, *Letters of C. S. Lewis*, 365; italics in original.

6. Neuhaus, *Death on a Friday Afternoon*, 260.

Sources

Bailey, Kenneth E. *Finding the Lost: Cultural Keys to Luke 15.* St. Louis, Mo.: Concordia, 1992.

———. *Poet and Peasant and Through Peasant Eyes: A Literary-Cultural Approach to the Parables in Luke.* Grand Rapids, Mich.: William B. Eerdmans, 1983.

Barclay, William. *The Parables of Jesus.* Louisville, Ky.: Westminster John Knox Press, 1970.

Benson, Ezra Taft. *The Teachings of Ezra Taft Benson.* Salt Lake City: Bookcraft, 1988.

Clark, J. Reuben, Jr. *"As Ye Sow."* Brigham Young University Speeches of the Year, Provo, Utah, 3 May 1955.

Collected Discourses. Edited and compiled by Brian H. Stuy. 5 vols. Salt Lake City: B.H.S. Publishing, 1992.

Conference Report. Salt Lake City: The Church of Jesus Christ of Latter-day Saints, April 1929; October 1936; April 1973; October 1976; October 1979; October 1980; October 1982; October 1984; October 1992; October 2000.

Hinckley, Gordon B. "Prophet Returns to Beloved England." *Church News,* 2 September 1995.

Holland, Jeffrey R. *However Long and Hard the Road.* Salt Lake City: Deseret Book, 1985.

Hultgren, Arland. *The Parables of Jesus.* Grand Rapids, Mich.: William B. Eerdmans, 2000.

Hymns of The Church of Jesus Christ of Latter-day Saints. Salt Lake City: The Church of Jesus Christ of Latter-day Saints, 1985.

Hymns: The Church of Jesus Christ of Latter-day Saints. Salt Lake City: Deseret Book, 1948.

Jeremias, Joachim. *The Parables of Jesus.* Upper Saddle River, N.J.: Prentice Hall, 1972.

Kimball, Spencer W. *The Miracle of Forgiveness.* Salt Lake City: Bookcraft, 1969.

Lee, Harold B. *Decisions for Successful Living.* Salt Lake City: Deseret Book, 1973.

Lewis, C. S. *Letters of C. S. Lewis.* Edited by Walter Hooper. Rev. ed. San Diego: Harcourt Brace & Co., 1993.

———. *Mere Christianity.* New York: Touchstone, 1996.

MacArthur, John F., Jr. *The Gospel According to Jesus.* Rev. ed. Grand Rapids, Mich.: Zondervan, 1994.

Marshall, I. Howard. *The Gospel of Luke: A Commentary on the Greek Text.* Grand Rapids, Mich.: William B. Eerdmans, 1978.

Maxwell, Neal A. *"For the Power Is in Them."* Salt Lake City: Deseret Book, 1970.

McConkie, Bruce R. *The Mortal Messiah.* 4 vols. Salt Lake City: Deseret Book, 1979–81.

McKay, David O. *Gospel Ideals.* Salt Lake City: Improvement Era, 1953.

Morris, Leon. *The Gospel According to St. Luke: An Introduction and Commentary.* Grand Rapids, Mich.: Eerdmans, 1974.

Neuhaus, Richard John. *Death on a Friday Afternoon.* New York: Basic Books, 2000.

The New Jerome Biblical Commentary. Edited by Raymond E. Brown,

Joseph A. Fitzmyer, and Roland E. Murphy. Englewood Cliffs, N.J.: Prentice Hall, 1990.

Nouwen, Henri J. M. *The Return of the Prodigal Son.* New York: Doubleday, 1992.

Oaks, Dallin H. "'Judge Not' and Judging." *Ensign,* August 1999.

Packer, Boyd K. *"That All May Be Edified."* Salt Lake City: Bookcraft, 1982.

Praise! Our Songs and Hymns. Grand Rapids, Mich.: Zondervan, 1979.

Rice, Richard. "Biblical Support for a New Perspective." In Clark Pinnock, Richard Rice, John Sanders, William Hasker, and David Basinger, *The Openness of God.* Downers Grove, Illinois: InterVarsity Press, 1994.

Smith, Joseph. *Teachings of the Prophet Joseph Smith.* Sel. Joseph Fielding Smith. Salt Lake City: Deseret Book, 1976.

Smith, Joseph F. *Gospel Doctrine.* Salt Lake City: Deseret Book, 1971.

Thielicke, Helmut. *The Waiting Father: Sermons on the Parables of Jesus.* New York: Harper & Brothers, 1959.

Volf, Miroslav. *Exclusion and Embrace: A Theological Exploration of Identity, Otherness, and Reconciliation.* Nashville: Abingdon Press, 1996.

Webster, Noah. *Webster's American Dictionary of the English Language.* 1828. Reprint. San Francisco: Foundation for American Christian Education, 1985.

Yancey, Philip. *The Jesus I Never Knew.* Grand Rapids, Mich.: Zondervan, 1995.

INDEX